Ways We Want Our Class To Be

Class Meetings that Build Commitment to Kindness and Learning

Ideas from the
Child Development Project

D<small>EVELOPMENTAL</small> S<small>TUDIES</small> C<small>ENTER</small>

DEVELOPMENTAL STUDIES CENTER

2000 Embarcadero, Suite 305
Oakland, CA 94606
(800) 666-7270
(510) 533-0213

ACKNOWLEDGMENTS

[1] Excerpt from *A Rocket in My Pocket: The Rhymes and Chants of Young Americans* by Carl Withers. © 1948 by Carl Withers. Reprinted by permission of Henry Holt and Co., Inc.

[2] "Poor Substitute" by Kalli Dakos reprinted with permission of Simon & Schuster Books for Young Readers, an imprint of Simon & Schuster Children's Publishing Division, from *If You're Not Here, Please Raise Your Hand* by Kalli Dakos. © 1990 by Kalli Dakos.

Contents

Part Two: Examples of Class Meetings

That's a Plan!

Planning and decision-making meetings can help students establish ways they want to treat each other, activities they want to do together, and things they want to learn.

How Are We Doing?

Check-in meetings let students reflect on how they're treating each other, what they're learning, and how well they're meeting their goals.

What's the Problem?

Sometimes it's enough to ask the question and let students talk about it with a check-in format. Sometimes a direct problem-solving approach is in order.

Class Meetings Checklist

Preface

*t*HE IDEAS in this guide have been distilled over many years and from many people who have worked to create caring communities in their schools and classrooms. Over the past decade, hundreds of teachers, administrators, parents, and children have collaborated with the Child Development Project (CDP) to make schools places where students care about each other and care about learning.

The Child Development Project

CDP is a comprehensive school-change effort to help elementary schools become inclusive communities and stimulating, supportive places to learn—because research shows that in order for children to reach their fullest social and academic potential they need

- close and caring relationships with their peers and teachers;
- opportunities to practice and benefit from prosocial values;
- challenging, relevant curriculum; and
- close cooperation and communication between families and school staff.

The CDP approach to creating such a learning community is multifaceted: it incorporates constructivist learning theory, cooperative learning techniques, classroom and schoolwide community-building strategies, and classroom management that helps students develop self-control and commitment to fundamental values such as fairness, kindness, and responsibility.

Class meetings, as described in this guide, are just one component of the staff development and materials that CDP offers to schools and teachers who want to promote children's ethical and social development, as well as their intellectual development. Other components include values-rich elementary and middle school literature-based reading programs that enlarge children's understanding of the world and their place in it; guides to cooperative learning that include classroom vignettes and lesson examples; and a collection of biweekly home activities that engage families in their children's learning. Videotapes made in CDP pilot schools show these components in action.

Acknowledgments

We would like to thank all those who contributed to this guide, especially the teachers who have given us invaluable insights from their own experience using the CDP approach to class meetings. Among them are Mary Ash, Karen Cailotto, Laurel Cress, Lynn Dames, Marcia Davis, Cynthia Evans, Sharon Friedman, Laura Havis, Brenda Henderson, Lynda Kamrath, Nancy Kasting, Carole Lewis, Louise Lotz, Judi Moncrief, Nancy Myers, Marsha Nichols, Donna Nordin, Nancy Noto, Lincoln Olbrycht, Ed Piñon, Linda Rayford, Joan Sfakianos, Cathy Sweeney, Margie Ura, and Judy Vowels. Many others contributed to writing this guide, including Fran Chamberlain, Stanley Rutherford, Peter Shwartz, and Dorothy Steele; but it was Anne Goddard and Cindy Litman who wrestled this book to the ground. Lynn Murphy was the book's editor; Alice Klein was the copy editor. Allan Ferguson managed its desktop design and production. The cover design is by Visual Strategies. The Child Development Project is directed by Eric Schaps, and Marilyn Watson is the CDP Program Director.

Funding to support the development, piloting, and dissemination of the Child Development Project has been provided by the following:

The William and Flora Hewlett Foundation
The Annenberg Foundation, Inc.
Center for Substance Abuse Prevention, Substance Abuse and Mental Health Services Agency, U.S. Department of Health and Human Services
DeWitt Wallace–Reader's Digest Fund, Inc.
The Robert Wood Johnson Foundation
The Pew Charitable Trusts
Anonymous Donor
Stuart Foundations
The John D. and Catherine T. MacArthur Foundation
Louise and Claude Rosenberg, Jr.
The Danforth Foundation
The San Francisco Foundation

Introduction

Creating a Community for Kindness and Learning

*e*SSENTIALLY, class meetings are times to talk—a forum for students and teacher to gather as a class to reflect, discuss issues, or make decisions about ways they want their class to be. Class meetings are not a forum for teachers to make pronouncements or impart decisions. Neither are they tribunals for students to judge one another. The teacher's role in these meetings is to create an environment in which students can see that their learning, their opinions, and their concerns are taken seriously. The students' role in these meetings is to participate as valuable and valued contributors to the classroom community.

Class meetings like these take time—time that never gets built into curriculum frameworks or district guidelines. Class meetings also take faith—faith that kids who may never have assumed responsibility for their learning and behavior are capable of doing so. And class meetings take practice, if only so that everyone comes to know what to expect.

Even given these demands, increasing numbers of teachers are making the time and taking the risks that class meetings require. Perhaps these teachers have found that sharing the load leaves everyone with more energy for learning and enjoying one another.

This is consonant with reports from the hundreds of teachers who have worked with the Child Development Project over the past decade. These teachers have used class meetings for a variety of purposes, finding the benefits of such meetings to include the following:

■ Class meetings help students establish and enjoy their own developing competence by encouraging them to set goals together and reflect upon their progress in achieving those goals.

■ Class meetings enhance students' sense of belonging and responsibility to the classroom by providing opportunities for them to express opinions and contribute to class decisions.

■ Class meetings help students gain an understanding of the meaning and importance of norms of fairness, kindness, and responsibility.

■ Class meetings help students gain greater understanding of themselves and others by providing a supportive environment in which they feel "safe" discussing personal interests, concerns, plans, and feelings.

■ Class meetings help students build a commitment to their role as learners by providing them with time to reflect on their learning and ways to contribute to decisions about it.

How to Use This Book

In the pages that follow, we will see how teachers use class meetings for everything from planning for a substitute to planning for a science unit. We will see how students can use class meetings to set class goals and monitor their progress in achieving them, to reflect on accumulated learning, and to solve common problems such as teasing, cliques, and "my friends won't let me play."

PART ONE: **Why, When, and How to Use Class Meetings** describes general purposes for class meetings, ways to establish an inviting environment for class meetings, and strategies for facilitating class meeting discussions.

PART TWO: **Examples of Class Meetings** is a collection of guidelines for fourteen meetings that cover typical subjects for class consideration. These guidelines can be used as templates, departure points, or both—whatever fits your own students and your own style of building community in your classroom.

PART ONE

Why, When, and How to Use Class Meetings

Purposes of Class Meetings

CLASS MEETINGS usually serve one or more of the following purposes: to plan and make decisions, to "check in," and to solve problems or raise awareness. Both academic and social issues are appropriate topics for consideration. Depending on their purpose, class meetings can be a regularly scheduled part of the school day or week or can occur as needed. Their versatility makes them a valuable classroom management tool — one that helps students actively contribute to their academic and social learning.

Planning and Decision-Making Meetings

*P*LANNING MEETINGS and decision-making meetings, in which students participate in charting a course of action for the classroom community, are suitable for both academic and class management purposes. For example, on the academic side you might hold a series of class meetings to have students help plan their next unit of study in science, and for class management purposes you might call a meeting to help students prepare for the eventuality of having a substitute teacher.

Ask Yourself These Questions When Setting a Topic

Whether your focus is to be academic or social, consider the following questions when setting a topic for a planning or decision-making meeting:

■ Is the topic open-ended, inviting participation from all children?

■ Is there really room for different ideas and viewpoints?

■ Do you really want student input, or are you calling the meeting to tell students what's what and to let them discuss it, *even though the outcome or expectation has already been decided—by you?*

Last year, my class buddied with a kindergarten class. At the end of the year, our class talked about whether we should do something special for the kindergarten class. They decided that they wanted to have a beach party. Now, we're *nowhere* near the beach. I asked them, 'What do you mean? Do you want to take a bus to the beach?' They said no, they wanted to make a beach at school. To myself I was thinking, 'Lordy,' but they went about it—they made a beach at the school by bringing in inflatable pools, and beach toys, and games from home. They made palm trees and pasted them on the real trees. They worked on it on their lunch breaks; they got together after school and made lists of toys and who would bring what.

Before, I would have been saying, 'No, no, no—let's do it this way. Let's just get some watermelon and eat it outside under the trees, neatly, and that will be that.' But I supported them. They know now that I'll be in their corner, that I will let them be creative. It's really opened things up in the classroom for them to know that they can go somewhere with their ideas, and I'll support them if I can."

When students brainstorm all the particular "ways we want our class to be," they begin the process of deciding what's important in a class that values kindness and learning.

- Will the children be able to act on their ideas or suggestions?

- Are you willing to support decisions made by the children even though you feel they might fail?

These questions frame the fundamental qualities of effective planning meetings and suggest the essential reasons for having class meetings—that is, to give students the experience of actively and responsibly helping to make decisions that affect their life in school. If you predetermine the decision that you want to extract from a "decision-making" meeting, or if you have a plan in mind and want to shepherd students into endorsing it, then they will not experience the benefits of being trusted to shape ideas and outcomes themselves. Moreover, they will quickly catch on to the rubber-stamp nature of such meetings and discount them or resist participating.

One day, about two months into the school year, we were having a discussion about how we wanted to run the class, and Maggie spoke up and said, 'You ask us what we want to do and we tell you and then you say, "No, no, no, we can't do that."' That little Maggie made me realize that I wasn't really giving them responsibility and then I realized that I had to take the plunge. My grandmother always said, if you ask a question, you better be ready to deal with the answer. So I recognized that I had to show them that I really respected their voice. There was a tremendous change in the classroom after that. They came to feel that they were really listened to."

Leave Room for Mistakes

Similarly, students need to learn how to learn from their mistakes—which means that you need to give them the leeway to do so (short of allowing students to plan anything dangerous or clearly unfeasible). Even if their plans don't turn out quite as expected, students will have gained the sense of autonomy that comes with being trusted to make decisions—and the corresponding sense of commitment to implementing their own plan. Both success and failure can lead to growth: students will learn how to think things through, adapt to circumstances, deal with setbacks or disappointment, take pride in their efforts, and celebrate their successes.

Beginning-of-the-Year Planning Meetings

Guidelines for several types of planning and decision-making class meetings are outlined in the second part of this book. Many of the examples deal with issues that arise at the beginning of the school year, a time when planning meetings serve a particularly valuable function by helping you to establish students' shared responsibility for the tenor of classroom life.

Planning-Our-Learning Meetings

Giving students a role in choosing what to learn about is another important way to build their autonomy and responsibility—but it's also a much bigger responsibility for you than simply proceeding through a textbook. It means making sure that students see connections and understand the importance of what they are learning, that they have or can get research resources, and that they learn about *how* to learn as well as about the subjects themselves. The payoff is a big one, though, because you are helping students experience themselves as real learners—people with questions and ways to answer them. Even when the curriculum is set by the district or state, you can give students many opportunities to exercise choice—for example, where to start, how much time to spend on each topic, what aspects of a topic to focus on.

Check-In Meetings

*C*HECK-IN MEETINGS can be about how the class is managing its behavior or about what students are learning. They can be a scheduled, anticipated part of a school day or week, or they can take place in a more summary way—at the end of a unit of study or semester of working together, for example. In any case, the point of check-in meetings is to reflect. Encourage students to celebrate what they have learned, evaluate how they have worked together, reflect on the outcome of an effort, and report on successes or problems. (But guide students away from using these meetings as their sole recourse for airing or dealing with their problems.)

If check-in meetings are worked into the fabric of daily or weekly classroom life, they can provide children with a sustained experience of their class as a dynamic, caring community. In addition, the regularity of these meetings will help students become familiar and comfortable with the class meeting process itself, so that they will be well prepared to successfully participate in class meetings called for other purposes.

General Check-In Meetings

Some examples of check-in meetings offered in the second section of this guide demonstrate the power of asking the broad questions "How are we doing?" and "What are we learning?" So, for instance, if students have determined in September "Ways We Want Our Class to Be," by January at the latest they should have a meeting evaluating "Is This the Way We Want to Be?"

Checking In on Specifics

Other examples in Part Two are of more specifically focused check-in meetings in which students evaluate the outcome of a particular plan or activity, which can help them become better planners and more responsible for their own behavior. If students have planned, for example, how to get along with a substitute, let them compare their plans with the reality and then perhaps make new plans or a new resolve.

Problem-Solving and Consciousness-Raising Meetings

*P*ERHAPS the most important point to emphasize about class meetings is that they are *not* synonymous with problem solving: if the classroom community comes together for discussion only when there is a problem to deal with, enthusiasm for such gatherings will quickly wane—especially since most "problems" tend to involve student misbehavior. Nonetheless, problem-solving meetings do serve a valuable purpose and pose some unique opportunities.

Focus on Solutions—Not Culprits

When students participate in discussing and resolving problems that affect their classroom community—with the focus always on solutions, not culprits—they come to share responsibility for aspects of the classroom life that might otherwise have been

Kindergarten children offer and consider ideas about how to interrupt each other less often during the morning circle.

> "Our class goes outside every day after lunch, but by the time they choose up teams, all the time to play is gone. So they decided during a class meeting that they would just split up into teams rather than spend time choosing them. And they did that, but the teams weren't very even, so one team was up at bat for the whole time and the other team didn't get a chance to get up. So they set up two innings and they asked me to tell them when half the time was up, and then it would be time for the other team to get up. They came up with that idea themselves . . . These experiences have shown them that they can do it for themselves. These solutions would not have worked if I had suggested them and imposed them."

borne solely by the teacher. Through such discussions, students can become more aware of why some actions are problematic (they simply might not recognize the hurtfulness of a particular behavior), perhaps become more reflective about their own behavior, gain a heightened sensitivity toward the feelings and perspectives of others, and become invested in solutions they have arrived at themselves. As students become experienced in perspective taking and conflict resolution, they will be able to apply these skills on their own and in settings other than the classroom.

This points to why these meetings are also referred to as "consciousness-raising" meetings: often they deal with general problem areas or behavior, not specific incidents. In many cases, these class discussions might not lead to explicit, concrete solutions, but will help ameliorate problem situations by raising students' awareness of how to see another's point of view and how to treat each other in more fair, kind, and responsible ways. This doesn't mean you should expect miraculous transformations, however—students may be able to articulate how they should treat each other, but it can often take a while for them to apply this learning. Keep in mind that *awareness* is the important first step in changing behavior, and therefore raising awareness is valuable in itself.

When Is a Problem Suitable for a Class Meeting?

Not all problems are suitable for whole-class discussion, and you will want to think about the following questions when considering whether an issue should be addressed in a class meeting:

- Is this an issue that can be discussed in a climate of trust, ensuring the safety of each child?

- Can the group's collective energy be directed toward finding solutions to problems, not consequences for actions? Or might the meeting turn into a "kangaroo court"?

- Does this issue affect all of the children or most of them? Would everyone benefit from considering it? Or does it involve only a few children, for whom it would be more appropriate to handle the matter privately? For example, a dispute between two children over a book would not warrant calling a class meeting—but if a general pattern of such disputes begins to emerge throughout the class, you might want to have a meeting about "sharing" or to revisit students' agreed-upon class norms for how to treat each other.

- If the meeting will address an issue or incident that concerns specific students, do all the parties involved agree to have the problem taken to the class, and will all parties be present?

- Is this the best time to address the problem? Sometimes a spontaneous class meeting to deal with an immediate problem can be very effective, especially if the problem is recurring, affects everyone, and has been the subject of previous discussion. If emotions are running high, however, you might want to postpone a class discussion until the problem can be dealt with in a less charged atmosphere.

Children are usually willing to talk as long as they know that you're willing to listen and to reason with them . . . In the past, instead of meeting to see if we could work out a problem, I would have simply imposed a penalty and told students that their behavior was wrong. The current way is much harder in that you have to spend the time talking to kids and working it out, but it may be easier in the long run because I'll get rid of the problem instead of just the symptom. Maybe the problem will be gone by March instead of continuing for the whole year. And maybe they'll learn something that will be important to them in their lives."

With issues like teasing, students need opportunities to take each other's perspectives and think about their personal contribution to the problem and its solution.

All of these considerations underscore what should be the salient feature of problem-solving meetings: that they be forums in which students work together to at least consider and perhaps agree on solutions for problems in their classroom community.

Problem-Solving and Consciousness-Raising Meetings

The second section of this guide offers a general structure for a problem-solving meeting, as well as two examples of how specific issues might be addressed. The emphasis in all these meetings is on perspective taking and reaching shared understandings or solutions.

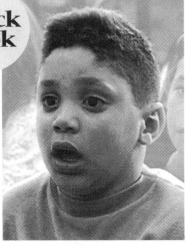

Quick Look

This preview of the class meetings outlined in Part Two provides concrete examples of the three types of meetings described in the previous pages.

Planning and Decision-Making Meetings

Here We Are! This meeting is for children in kindergarten and first grade, especially those who may be experiencing a formal school setting for the first time. It introduces the idea of the classroom as a community, builds on children's intrinsic motivation to learn, and lets the teacher in on some of the personalities in the classroom. *Page 50*

Ways We Want Our Class to Be. This two-session meeting invites students' thoughtful participation in establishing class rules or norms. Rather than having students experience class rules as a list dictated by the teacher, this meeting lets students think through the reasons for setting norms for their own behavior, then structures a

way for them to set their own norms— norms they are intrinsically committed to respecting. (This guideline comes in two versions, one to suit the abilities of children just starting school and one to suit the greater experience and maturity of older students.) *Page 53/Page 57*

Class Name. A simple means to building students' sense of community is to let them choose a class name. In doing so, students gain appreciation for the diversity of their peers, develop skills in achieving consensus, and arrive at a commonly held sense of identity in their chosen class name. *Page 63*

Back-to-School Night/Open House. This meeting topic provides another vehicle for building students' sense of unity and identity as a class body. Students help plan how they want their class to be presented at a Back-to-School Night or Open House, which encourages them to think about the class's unique character and their shared sense of community. *Page 67*

Substitutes. At some point during the school year most classes have a substitute teacher—which can be a trying experience for both the substitute and the students. This class meeting asks students to think about that prospect, from their own and from the visiting teacher's perspective, and to plan how to make this a positive experience for everyone. *Page 72*

Choosing to Learn. Variations of this class meeting can be used over and over during the year—for example, to help students choose units of study, book groups to join, or the topic for a small-group report. *Page 76*

Check-In Meetings

Is This the Way We Want to Be?

At least a couple of times during the year, make time for students to evaluate their behavior against the goals they set for themselves at the beginning of the year. What are they doing well? What would they like to improve? (Like its prerequisite meeting, "Ways We Want Our Class to Be," this guideline comes in a version for primary students and a version for older students.) *Page 82/Page 86*

What Did We Learn? It is important

to help children see themselves as learners and to build their appreciation of the many ways and the many things they are learning. A brief daily or weekly conversation about "What did we learn?" can build students' recognition of and pride in their accomplishments, reveal student concerns that the teacher may want to address, and reinforce students' sense of their classroom as a community of learners. This meeting can also be used at the end of a specific unit of study. *Page 90*

How Did It Go with the Substitute? This meeting is a

follow-up to the planning meeting described above, "Substitutes," in which students developed a plan for how to "deal with" substitute teachers. This check-in meeting can be held after each time the class has a substitute. The purpose here is not to find out who-did-what-wrong-to-whom, but to encourage students to reflect on their *plan*—and to learn the valuable lesson that even the best plans should be reviewed periodically and adapted wisely. *Page 94*

Problem-Solving and Consciousness-Raising Meetings

Problem Solving. This example does not deal with a specific topic, as do the other guidelines offered in this book, but is more of a blueprint for how to use a class meeting to address "problem" topics in general. This guideline establishes the approach and the essential elements of a problem-solving meeting; a teacher can then build on these suggestions to most appropriately address an issue at hand. *Page 100*

My Friends Won't Let Me Play.

Young children often need help working through their experiences of social conflict, such as the issue addressed in this guideline. When children bring problems to teachers, such as "My friends won't let me in their game," the "tattling" often reflects a genuine problem that needs to be addressed. By exploring with the class the context of such complaints, teachers will help children develop a more mature and sympathetic approach to social relationships. *Page 106*

Cliques. Children in upper grades also experience their own, usually more intricate, forms of social conflict. In keeping with the increasingly sophisticated relationships and difficulties experienced by older children, this guideline is an example of a more in-depth approach to discussing and resolving conflict. *Page 109*

The Environment for Class Meetings

SUCCESSFUL class meetings require an encouraging environment: students must feel comfortable expressing their opinions—confident that their ideas will be treated respectfully by peers and teacher alike. Such an environment rests largely on each student's sense of connection to the classroom community, a teacher's facilitation skills, and students' familiarity with the class meeting process. For students who have rarely been encouraged to express their opinions or trusted to hold productive and respectful discussions, it may take some time and practice before they do so smoothly and openly. In the meantime, you can attend to a few practical details and preliminaries to help create an environment that invites participation.

Creating a Comfortable Atmosphere

a SAFE AND trusting atmosphere within the classroom is important for the success of most learning activities, and class meetings are no exception—in fact, meetings can be a particularly intimidating forum for many people, child or adult. While it may take time for students to feel truly at ease expressing themselves in meetings, you can help establish some level of comfort by simply helping students get to know each other at the beginning of the year. When you do begin holding meetings, start with short meetings and modest objectives; tell students, and demonstrate, that you value all their answers and expect them to treat each other respectfully.

Getting-to-Know-You Activities

Before holding the first class meeting, you will want to give students numerous opportunities to "meet" one another informally through activities such as those described below. As a member of the classroom community, it is important that you also participate in the activities and be "introduced" to your class. You may want some activities to have school-related content and others to be just for fun.

- **Add-on Graffiti Boards.** At the top of bulletin boards or large pieces of paper around the room, sentences or phrases such as "I like school when . . ." or "Favorite Books" are posted. Students and teacher then write endings or responses to the headings.

- **Artifacts.** For this activity, an "artifact" is an item connected with someone or something important or memorable in a person's life. Students and teacher bring in an artifact, preferably in a paper bag or other container that hides it from view. Each person tells the story behind the artifact and then shows it to the rest of the class. (Artifacts are also effective as a partner interview topic; see below.)

- **Class Data Base.** Students and teacher make a class chart or graph showing information about individuals' hobbies, birthdays, favorite food or book, and so on. (The data base should not include topics, such as weight or height, that might cause negative feelings for those at either end of a range or topics that students might feel they need to embellish, such as bedtimes.)

- **Find Your Match.** Students and teacher form groups with others in the class who share a particular attribute, such as the same birthday month, or a particular preference (for example, all those who choose the same animal picture or quote from a children's book could form a group). The group members then explore what else they have in common, also discovering their dissimilarities and diversity in the process.

> "I got a lot of positive comments from parents about the unity builders [getting-to-know-you activities]. Parents said things like, 'I'm surprised how well my daughter knows her classmates. She knows all about what they like and dislike. We'll be walking in a department store and she'll say, "Beth is crazy about polka dots," or we'll be walking in a grocery store and she'll say, "So-and-so brings raisins to school every day and he gives some to all the kids."' Parents felt that it was really nice for their kids to know other kids so well."

■ **Forced Choice.** This is another activity that helps students appreciate how they are alike and how they are different: students and teacher move between two (or more) different areas in the room according to how they answer each in a series of questions. For example, the teacher might ask:

- Would you rather read a biography or write an autobiography?
- Would you rather visit Antarctica or Hawaii?
- Would you rather draw a picture, act out a story, or sing a song?
- Would you rather learn about insects or earthquakes?
- Would you rather play softball, piano, or chess?

■ **I Am Thinking of Someone.** Students try to guess the classmate (or teacher) being described by a series of hints about the person. Descriptions of positive acts and personal preferences, such as "someone who likes to play with puppets and shares them with others," will contribute to children's appreciation of each other.

■ **Partner Interviews.** Partners take turns interviewing each other about a particular topic introduced by the teacher and then write and/or draw about what they have learned about their partner. Students could work individually after the interviews, or partners might collaborate on the writing and drawing. Students then tell the class what they learned about their partners. This is a good activity to do several times at the beginning of the year, switching partners each time, and then frequently throughout the year. Topics can be school- or non-school-related:

- *Are You Curious?* Partners interview each other about things they want to learn.

Students need lots of opportunities to get to know each other—early in the year and throughout the year. Their sense of comfort with each other in class meetings is directly related to the experiences they have working and talking together in a variety of contexts.

- *Helping Hands.* Students find out about a time their partner did something to help someone, and then they draw a picture of their partner's story inside an outline of the partner's hand.
- *I Can.* Partners interview each other about things they like to do or can do well.
- *I Remember.* Partners find out each other's memories of when they went on a picnic, rode on a bus, lost a tooth, etc.
- *Talking Artifacts.* Students bring an item connected with someone or something important or memorable in their lives, such as a photograph of a pet, a letter from a grandparent, a favorite toy, etc. Their partners ask questions to learn the story of the object.
- *We Are Alike/We Are Different.* Partners make Venn diagrams or other graphic representations of ways they are similar and ways they are different.

- *What Did You Learn?* Partners find out favorite things they learned from a book, activity, or unit of study.

- **Photograph Display.** The teacher takes Polaroid (or other) snapshots of students and posts them on a bulletin board labeled with students' names and other information of interest. Depending upon their age and writing skills, students can create their own displays for the board or for a class book. For example, individual students might choose photos that interest them and write a caption, or partners might interview each other and paste their partner's picture on a star and write information about their partner on each point of the star.

- **Webbing.** With the class (and teacher) seated in a circle, a student holds a ball of yarn and tells the class his or her name and a fact about him- or herself. Holding the end of the yarn, that student then rolls the ball of yarn across the circle to another child, who repeats the process. As the class members introduce themselves and roll the ball to other students, the ball unwinds into a web of yarn connecting everyone.

Establishing Ground Rules

aNOTHER important aspect of creating an environment for successful class meetings is the establishment of ground rules that are simply "givens"—behaviors that are necessary if students are to have productive discussions. Before you hold your first class meeting, explain the purposes of class meetings, and then present some ground rules that will help the class achieve those purposes. (With older students or students with previous experience doing class meetings, you might choose to let them be involved in creating these ground rules, but for young or inexperienced students it will be more efficient simply to lay out the ground rules yourself and let the students get quickly into the actual business of the meeting.)

To help students understand the rationale for ground rules, focus their attention on the principle that all group members should be able to freely and fairly participate in the class meeting process, and ask them to think about what that might require. When they have a conversation with someone, how do they treat the other person, and how do they like to be treated? How might this translate into ground rules for a class meeting discussion? Give students a chance to discuss these questions, and then suggest several basic ground rules, such as the following:

■ One person speaks at a time.

■ Listen to each other.

■ Allow each other to disagree.

■ No put-downs.

■ No finger-pointing or blaming.

The goal of the ground rules, of course, is to help students treat one another fairly, respectfully, and considerately in class meetings, as in all interactions.

Listening and Getting a Turn to Speak

One of the most difficult aspects of facilitating any meeting, with children or adults, is to assure fair access to the floor. This will be a challenge especially with young children, who may have trouble taking turns, and with children who see discussions as an opportunity to vie for the teacher's attention.

It is important, then, to help students see that class meetings are about *them* coming to understandings as a group, and that this requires them not to hog the floor and to speak and listen *to each other*. Because many children see teachers as their primary audience in discussions, helping students speak to each other—with or without you as an intermediary—is an important facilitation role.

Some upper-grade teachers have worked with their students to eliminate the practice of raising hands to be called on to speak. Instead, students respond directly to each other, monitoring for themselves who will speak next. It takes practice to achieve this level of discussion with large groups and in classrooms where everyone is conditioned to raising hands. Teachers find that initially they must help students redirect their comments from the teacher to other students and that students need practice in learning how to take turns in an open discussion.

In classes where raising hands is expected, the teacher can still call on students but help them direct their comments to each other, both with statements to that effect ("Please tell the class . . ." or "Please tell Jannie . . .") and with gestures to remind them (such as nodding toward the others in the room and redirecting one's own eyes away from the called-on student). And, of course, no students should have their hands raised while someone else is speaking.

With very young students, some teachers use a tangible reminder of whose turn it is to speak; for example, the child who has the floor holds an object, such as a teddy bear or a wand, then passes the object to the next speaker, and so on. Because this is a cumbersome way to have a discussion, it is best reserved only for early in the year when students may be unused to or out of practice waiting for a turn.

Regardless of the strategies you use to facilitate class meeting discussions, students will be most successful if they understand the purpose of such strategies: maintaining fair and considerate behavior so they can accomplish their goals for the meeting.

Avoiding Accusatory or Shaming Discussions

A ground rule such as "No finger-pointing or blaming" reminds students of a particularly *un*productive way to approach a problem. A possible risk of class meetings, especially problem-solving meetings, is that individual children will be unkindly treated or publicly shamed; this is particularly likely to happen to children who are unpopular or always "in trouble." While this probably can't be completely eliminated, the best preventative measure is to constantly cultivate an environment that is respectful of all individuals and that emphasizes the need to find solutions to problems, not culprits.

To this end, some teachers ask their students to discuss problems without naming names. While this might help in many situations, sometimes it is impractical or can exacerbate the problem. For example, young children often are simply unable to describe problems without referring to the specific people involved; and even when names aren't mentioned, children often know who is being referred to anyway. Also, cautioning children not to name names implies that the person not being named would be shamed if his or her transgression became public knowledge. But this needn't be the case. Part of creating a sense of community is learning to help one another participate fully, fairly, and responsibly in the life of the community—in other words, creating a shared understanding that "We all want to be good people and good students, and we'll all make mistakes as we strive for that goal, so we need to help each other be the best that we can be." The mistakes (problems, conflicts) that happen needn't be cause for shame, then, but cause for renewed effort and help.

Still, students *will* be embarrassed by their misdeeds, and it is therefore important to establish a class norm that focuses on solving problems rather than merely placing blame: that is, to treat one another respectfully while still dealing forthrightly with problems. Your own responses, of course, will provide an important and influential model for students.

Even Ground Rules Take Time

Remember that students will probably need to practice before they become comfortable with the class meeting process, including the ground rules. Review the ground rules before each meeting until students no longer need the reminder. (If you have students who have particular difficulty with the ground rules—for example, often interrupting or holding side conversations—you may need to work with them individually to plan together how to manage this behavior. An example: you might agree upon private signals that you will give them when they need to "rein themselves in.") Throughout the school year, encourage your students to suggest revisions or additions to the ground rules, based on their growing experience of class meetings and the etiquette of discussions.

> We tried having class meetings, we evaluated it, we tweaked it here and there. The students like it because, through the class meetings, they feel listened to and respected."

Physical Set-Up

*E*SSENTIALLY, in a class meeting students are having a conversation with each other. You want to encourage this conversation and help students understand that they can talk directly to each other, not just through you. The physical set-up of a meeting can in itself make this point by helping participants feel connected to each other: they need to be able to see each other, easily have eye-to-eye contact, and converse without having to shout. Many teachers have students sit in a circle—in chairs or on a rug (if furniture moving is involved, have students practice doing this quickly and quietly).

Think about your own placement in the group and what will help students think of you as a participant in this community meeting, rather than a focal point or discussion conduit. For example, you might change your placement within the group from meeting to meeting; or you might sit with the children at their level (perhaps on the floor with them rather than in a chair). Invite students' suggestions, as well, and experiment with the arrangement, thereby modeling for students the flexibility to thoughtfully make, reconsider, and revise a plan.

Duration of Meetings

*t*EACHERS often want to know how long class meetings should be, but there is no single answer to this—it depends upon the age and experience of the students, the topic(s) to be addressed, and the purpose of the meeting. Think situationally. For example, teachers and students who are new to class meetings might begin with short meetings and modest objectives; meetings with six-year-olds will be a lot shorter than meetings with sixth-graders; and end-of-day check-ins might last fifteen minutes, while trying to decide on class norms might take two or three hours spread over several meetings.

Your primary concern is to see that meetings are neither too long *nor* too short. You don't want meetings to sputter on after interest and engagement wane, but neither do you want the meeting to feel abridged or participants to feel frustrated because they didn't get a chance to express their viewpoints. This requires you to be flexible. For instance, you will need to be able to recognize when a brief check-in meeting has raised an important issue that requires a longer meeting devoted just to that issue (not necessarily at that time, however; the practice of recording "unfinished business" to be carried over to the next meeting allows you to close a meeting even though a solution has not been reached).

However long or short a meeting, allow time at the end for students to assess it: What went well? What could we do differently next time? What did we accomplish at this meeting? What needs to be carried over to the next meeting? Concluding with a brief evaluation invites children to reflect about the role of these meetings as well as their own contribution to them.

Discussion and Facilitation Strategies

THE BEST intentions to create an open, trusting atmosphere for class meetings can be frustrated if the class and teacher lack discussion skills or are unpracticed at reaching consensus. Class meetings require that the teacher function as a model, a listener, and a facilitator—accepting students' ideas and feelings, drawing students out, letting them air opinions, helping them see their classmates' perspectives, encouraging them to respond to each other, and prompting them to reflect on and extend their own thoughts. While leading such discussions is a skill that you will develop over time, there are some basic understandings and strategies worth starting with. Coupled with good will and practice, these strategies can help you and your students to establish patterns of comfortable discussion and decision making.

What the Teacher Models

*b*ECAUSE class meetings enable teachers to participate in the classroom community as a member as well as its leader, they are an ideal vehicle for teachers to model positive behaviors among equals. How you behave with your "less experienced colleagues" (i.e., your students) demonstrates how they should treat each other in their own collegial relationships. Your evident respect for all students' ideas—including your willingness to value the contributions of the shy, the less articulate, and the unpopular—lends significant integrity to the class norms about respect and fairness.

Likewise, such positive modeling can occur whenever you demonstrate thoughtful and fair treatment in approaching issues with your students. The way you help them organize alternative solutions or choices, the way you frame a discussion around a problem rather than its perpetrator, the way you show how much you value consensus

When the teacher models a willingness to explore ideas rather than impose them, students experience themselves as capable thinkers and problem solvers.

and collaboration—all will greatly inform students as to how they should behave in the moment and in the future.

Finally, it will be helpful if your students realize that meetings are not some artificial construct that applies only to their classroom lives. Share with your students your own adult experiences of meetings—discussions, negotiations, reflections, rethinking your own ideas and plans—showing them that the skills they can develop through class meetings are in themselves important life skills.

Questioning and Response Strategies

*Y*OUR ability to respond to students in a manner that catalyzes and extends discussion is key to the effectiveness of class meetings. This ability has to do not only with how you model listening skills, but also how you foster students' reasoning and communication skills. (Responsive dialogue has long been recognized as an important key to literacy, and your ability to listen to students and help them shape their ideas clearly can make class meetings an important center of language learning.) First and foremost, your questioning and response style must consistently reinforce that you are not looking for a "right" answer, but for *their* answers.

This invitational quality relies, in part, on what questions you pose and how you pose them. As with any class discussion, you will want to use open-ended questions that encourage students to go beyond their first notions and consider related issues, ideas, and alternatives. Sometimes this encouragement might simply be a matter of giving students time to reflect and respond, or sometimes you might need to reframe or refocus your questions to engage their thinking.

Wait Time

After asking a question, it is important to wait three to five seconds before accepting answers; this eliminates competition to be first with an answer and allows all students to assimilate the question and consider a response. If students aren't accustomed to "wait time," you might need to explain that you are giving everyone time to think, even if the pause seems awfully long at first. In this way you will explicitly underscore that you value thoughtfulness and that you consider their ideas worthwhile. Extending the wait time will increase the number of responses, the number of students responding, and the depth of students' responses.

> "Class meetings were difficult for me in the beginning, but now I feel more comfortable managing them. Practice has made me confident—and seeing the results."

It is also effective to use wait time after a student responds and before you speak again. Not only does this allow you to think about the student's answer and ponder your next move, but this short pause also gives students an important sign that you carefully consider their remarks. Wait time also often increases student-to-student interaction, as class members begin trying to clarify things for you or respond to each other in your silence; this promotes a true community discussion rather than a teacher-student question-and-answer session.

Follow-Up Questions

Even allowing for wait time, some questions fail to stimulate much conversation, and you will need to try another approach. For example, if the meeting topic concerns friendship, and the question "What is a friend?" seems too abstract for children, you might try another type of open-ended but more specific question, such as the following examples:

- *Personal connection:* "Think about your best friend or a friend you wish you had. What does your friend do? How does your friend treat you? What does your friend do that makes you feel good?" Questions that elicit personal stories often bring responses full of themes and ideas to be pursued in the ensuing discussion.

- *Compare and contrast:* "What's the difference between someone who isn't a friend and someone who is?"

- *Cause and effect:* "What do you do when you meet someone new and want to be that person's friend?"

- *Benefits and burdens:* "Are there some hard things, as well as good things, about having or being a friend?"

Also remember that you are part of this conversation, and perhaps offering a story of your own might get the discussion going. Just as knowing your students as individuals helps you feel connected to them, so do your students benefit from seeing you as a "real person" for whom these discussions and issues are also relevant.

Finally, always remember that this is a community discussion and that you needn't be the only member asking questions and probing the thinking of the others. Encourage students to talk *to each other*. They should feel free to respond to each other's statements, challenge each other's thinking, and ask each other follow-up questions—in a fair and respectful manner, of course.

How to Encourage and Manage Participation

*A*NOTHER aspect of facilitating a class meeting is using various "formats" to both encourage and manage broad student participation in the discussion. For example, a whole-group discussion might not be the best format if you have students who are reluctant to express their thoughts in front of the whole group. (In such cases, you don't want to force or cajole anyone into participating—just because some students don't often speak up, it doesn't mean that they aren't assimilating, thinking, and learning.) Conversely, you might encounter topics that generate such great interest it seems that *everyone* has an idea to share, and you will want to avoid having any students feel "left out" if they don't get a chance to voice their thoughts. Also, you always want to encourage student-to-student discussion and wean them from the notion that all communication must be channeled through the teacher.

The formats below allow you some versatility in structuring your class meetings, whether your purpose is to encourage quiet students, manage enthusiastic response, encourage peer interactions, or just elicit the widest and most productive participation possible. In addition to (or instead of) whole-class discussions, you can mix-and-match these formats to suit the nature of the topic and the "mood" of the class, or simply to add variety to students' experience of class meetings.

Brainstorming

This is a tool that you might already use with your class (and will certainly use frequently for class meetings), but it's worth reviewing here in the context of encouraging and managing participation. During brainstorming, students are asked to offer *any* ideas that come to mind about the given topic and to reserve comment or discussion about each other's ideas until later. Whether used in a whole-class or small-group discussion, brainstorming offers students a nonthreatening means of participation—everyone's ideas are invited, no one's ideas are critiqued, and everyone understands that these can be "take-a-chance," "tickle-some-new-thinking" ideas.

Small-Group Discussions

Having students break into small groups for discussion can be a vehicle for managing large topics. The groups could discuss the topic at hand and summarize their ideas for the whole group, thereby giving all group members a chance to express themselves but streamlining the idea-sharing in the whole-group setting. Or, if the main topic is multifaceted, each group could take on a particular aspect of the larger issue and then bring their part of it back to the whole group. At the same time, small-group discussions offer a smaller, safer scope of participation that can help draw quieter students into the conversation and elicit contributions that might otherwise not have been made in the larger group.

Partner Chats

Partner chats, in which students turn to a partner to discuss issues and solutions, are basically smaller versions of the small-group discussion and serve the same purposes. If a whole-group discussion becomes unwieldy because so many students have so much to say, then a partner chat gives everyone a chance to articulate and clarify their ideas and ensures that no one feels slighted. Also, less assertive students might feel safer exchanging ideas with just one person than with the whole group. Partner chats, like small-group discussions, also reinforce the value of student-to-student exchanges: they give students a chance to develop their skills in productive and respectful peer interaction, and they offer tangible evidence to students that class meetings are about *their* ideas, not about pleasing the teacher with the "right" ideas.

Partner chats are particularly useful when everybody wants to talk or when too few people are willing to volunteer.

Partner Idea List

This format explicitly encourages students to exercise and develop their listening and communication skills. With partner idea lists, students work in pairs to brainstorm, discuss, and reach consensus on ideas related to a given topic.

- Explain that you want partners to brainstorm with each other and record each other's ideas, without deciding whether they like the idea or not. (If you are working with younger students, keep in mind that although making lists is a natural way for young children to begin writing and some students may enjoy recording their ideas in writing, they should also be given the option to record their partners' ideas as drawings.)

- Encourage students to listen carefully to each other, especially since they are responsible for recording the ideas they are listening to. Ask that they refrain from interrupting, even if they get a really good idea while their partner is speaking.

- Then have partners discuss their lists, telling each other what they do or do not like about each idea (they can add new ideas that arise during this discussion, as well). Ask them to star the ideas that are most important to *both* partners.

After partners have made their lists, invite them to share their starred ideas with the whole group, and continue the class discussion from there.

Collected Ideas

A simple way to manage the collection of all the ideas that partners or small groups want to share is to begin by inviting one group to give one idea. Ask all other groups with a similar idea to raise their hands. Invite another group to offer a different idea. Ask all other groups with a similar idea to raise their hands—and so forth until all ideas have been heard.

Individual Reflection and Writing

At times you may want to use this format to help students think things through for themselves before engaging in a whole- or small-group discussion. Also, when discussions get particularly heated, a break for personal reflection and writing can help cool tempers and move students toward more reasoned, less emotional thinking and self-expression.

Consensus

*P*ERHAPS the most difficult aspect of class meetings is reaching consensus on decisions or solutions—and perhaps the most important thing to emphasize here is that many class meetings *won't* end neatly with a final decision or plan of action. Keep in mind that sometimes it is sufficient just to have brought up and discussed an issue, raising everyone's awareness about it.

But when the class *does* need to make a decision or resolve a problem, it is important that both teacher and students share a desire to reach consensus. When thirty-odd students are struggling with an issue, it can be tempting—for everyone involved—to seek the will of the majority by simply having students vote. The problem with voting, however, is that it tends to be a divisive experience that creates "winners" and "losers"—a distinction that significantly diminishes the sense of a caring community. The process of how a class arrives at a decisions is as important as what the final decision is, and the process of consensus building is more responsive than "majority rules" to the many voices within a group. The consensus-building process therefore not only reaffirms students' sense that their individual participation is meaningful and worthwhile, but also is invaluable in helping build their lifelong abilities of perspective taking, negotiation, and seeing compromise as a "winning" solution rather than a sign of weakness or failure.

What is consensus? Here are two useful definitions:

- Everyone can live with the decision, even if it's no one's first choice.
- "We keep giving ideas until nobody disagrees. If anybody disagrees, we give more ideas." (From a first-grader.)

Five Steps

How is such consensus to be achieved? Here is the consensus-building process reduced to its most essential elements (Steps Three and Four are elaborated later):

- STEP ONE: **Define the problem or issue in concrete terms.**
  - State the problem in a way that shows why it is a problem.
  - Tell why the problem concerns everyone or will benefit from everyone's help.
  - If necessary, define consensus so that everyone will know what the aim of the discussion is and at what point they will have been successful.
- STEP TWO: **Brainstorm solutions.**

Even first-graders understand consensus: "We keep giving ideas until nobody disagrees. If anybody disagrees, we give more ideas."

■ STEP THREE: Discuss solutions.

- Reduce the number of ideas and narrow the choices, if necessary.

■ STEP FOUR: Reach consensus.

- Guide the group toward resolution through combining, developing, or compromising on ideas.
- Determine whether consensus has been reached by asking students if they can live with the solution. If any answer that they can't, then consensus hasn't been reached.
- Be sure to talk about the experience with the class, and discuss what the group has learned that they can use the next time they try to reach consensus.
- Congratulate yourselves—reaching consensus *is* an achievement!

■ STEP FIVE: Evaluate the decision.

- At a later time discuss how well the decision worked or is working.

When students explain why an idea is appealing, they may be giving other children a fresh way to appreciate it and possibly build consensus around it.

Strategies for Narrowing Choices *(Step Three)*

After brainstorming solutions, the class may find itself faced with a very large range of alternatives from which to choose. Below are some strategies for helping students reduce their options to a manageable few.

■ **Benefits and Burdens.** Students explain what they consider the advantages and disadvantages of each idea (which helps students clarify their thinking and broaden their perspectives):

- Ask students to describe and explain what they see as the benefits and burdens that each option entails.

- Record students' ideas, and give students a few minutes to think about these perspectives.

- Ask whether this group of ideas helps students to eliminate or combine any of the options (a simple way to do this might be to move into one of the following strategies, which ask students to make such choices).

■ **Unlivable Only.** Students name the choices they can't live with, and explain why (which helps eliminate unpopular ideas and helps students clarify their thinking):

- Have each student state or write down the ideas he or she can't live with and why (you might find that students feel safer writing down their thoughts than stating them before the whole group).

- Cross out the "unlivable" ideas as students voice them; or, if students wrote down their ideas, read aloud and cross out the ideas that have been rejected.

- Then work with students to reach consensus on the remaining ideas—but if all the ideas have been rejected, work with students to brainstorm new options or amend previous options. For example, if some ideas have been rejected by only a very few students, perhaps those ideas can be modified so that everyone can live with them.

■ **Livable Only.** Students name all the choices they can live with (which highlights areas of common agreement and weeds out truly unlivable ideas):

- Read aloud each option, asking students to raise their hands if they can live with it. Make sure they understand that they can "vote" as many times as they like—if they can live with every idea, then they can raise their hands for every idea.

- For each option, count the number of raised hands and mark that number beside the idea.

- Then help students build consensus around the ideas that have the highest "livability scores."

■ **One "Why."** Students each choose one idea and explain why they chose it (which helps students clarify their thinking, eliminates unpopular ideas, and highlights deep disagreements):

- Have students each identify the one idea they prefer and explain why.

- Record each student's choice and reasoning, and eliminate any options that received no support.

- If the range of options still seems unwieldy, repeat this winnowing process, and help students reach consensus around the preferences that have emerged.

■ **Three Straws.** Students cast three straws (which eliminates all but a few choices, while also allowing students to express the strength of their preferences):

- Give each student three "straw votes" to distribute in any way he or she chooses—make sure students understand that they can cast all three votes for one option, one vote each for three different options, etc.

- Tally students' votes; only a few clear preferences will emerge, on which you can then help students reach consensus.

■ **Apply Criteria.** Students assess objective criteria that can be applied to the decision (which gives them common ground upon which to build a decision, even if they have different preferences):

- Help students identify objective criteria that affect the issue. For example, if the class is discussing where to go on a field trip, there are probably budgetary, logistical, or curriculum factors that might be taken into consideration.

- Use a simple matrix to assess the impact of these considerations, listing the options down one side and the criteria across the top, as in the example below. Then, as a group, mark where the options meet the listed criteria. If students suggest subjective criteria, such as "the field trip has to be fun," help them understand why those criteria are ineligible for this assessment (and perhaps draw up those considerations on a separate list of what students want from the trip). In the example below, going to the aquarium emerges as a likely decision purely on pragmatic grounds, without slighting the worth of the other options or individual students' preferences.

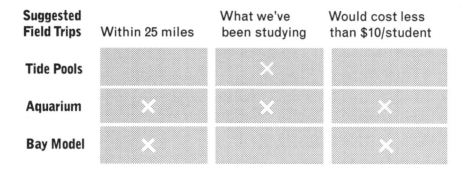

Suggested Field Trips	Within 25 miles	What we've been studying	Would cost less than $10/student
Tide Pools		X	
Aquarium	X	X	X
Bay Model	X		X

> This is different from what I might have done a few years ago because I would
> have told them what to do rather than asking them what we should do . . .
> When they have input, their commitment is different."

Strategies for Reaching Agreement *(Step Four)*

Once the number of options has been reduced, keep the process positive by helping students focus on their areas of agreement and build on alternatives so that they become more widely acceptable. Could an option be modified so that everyone can live with it? Could two ideas be combined into a version that satisfies the whole class? This stage of the consensus-building effort can prove the most challenging to the teacher-facilitator, as most students have little or no experience resolving these kinds of difficulties—they will *truly* be learning while doing. Even if the process becomes frustrating, model and explain how you value the skills of negotiation, perspective taking, and creative accommodation.

If the class gets bogged down and seems at an impasse, however, return to the brainstorming, discussion, and list-reduction process. Challenge the students to examine and extend their thinking: "Did we generate enough alternatives during our brainstorming? Are there other areas to explore? Did we overlook some criteria?" People's perspectives are often broader once they have wrestled with a problem, and students may well find new ideas when covering "old ground." (On the other hand, there may be times when the meeting has gone on long enough, continues to circle on itself, or has turned rancorous, and it is best to end the meeting and return to the topic at another time.)

Once the class has reached consensus, be sure to help students appreciate two aspects of this process: first, this outcome is based on those alternatives that *they* chose and, second, consensus represents a true *community* decision that is fully and appropriately respectful of everyone's ideas and feelings.

Troubleshooting

*i*N ANY whole-group discussion, especially those that are student-driven, it can be quite a challenge to keep things running smoothly. To wrap up this section on facilitation strategies, here are a few "troubleshooting" hints that might come in handy.

PROBLEM	ASK YOURSELF	TRY
Everybody talking	Is it because they are so interested?	Ask them to tell their idea to a partner.
	Is it because they are *not* interested?	Rephrase the question, or add interest to the topic, or drop it.
	Is it because they have not *heard* the topic?	Get their attention first, check your timing, review the ground rules, etc.
Nobody talking	Do they understand?	Rephrase the question, give more information.
	Are they interested?	Add interest, or drop it.
	Do they need to think more, to formulate their ideas?	Invite them to discuss the question with their partner or write individually about it.

PROBLEM	ASK YOURSELF	TRY
Side conversations or interference	Is the discussion hitting "too close to home"?	Give students time to write individually about the topic, or table the discussion.
	Is the discussion of no concern to them?	Acknowledge the fact, and shorten the meeting if possible.
	Do they have a problem with self-control?	Help them develop self-control. Work out a "plan for class meetings" in advance with individuals who usually have a problem. Help them evaluate their progress.
Shocking or "funny" or "stupid" statements	Is it really in order to get attention? Or could it be a method used to cover up for feeling embarrassed?	Deal with this directly. Keep your sense of humor! Sometimes you may decide to have a private talk with the "offender," particularly if this is a pattern.
	Is it from an inability to express themselves clearly?	Rephrase, "Do you mean . . .?" Or ask them to rephrase— and give them time.
Someone too disruptive to stay in the group	How can I stop the behavior and not build resentment? How can I help the person take responsibility for his or her own behavior?	Ask the person to leave the group until she or he is able to return without being disruptive.

PART
TWO

Examples of
Class Meetings

THE FOLLOWING PAGES offer guidelines for class meetings structured around common classroom concerns, events, or problems. A few are written for specific grades, while the others can be adapted for a range of grades and ages. In some guidelines, variations are suggested depending on whether the meeting is to be used with younger or older students. Each class meeting guideline follows the same basic pattern:

- Description of the topic

- Special considerations for the teacher to bear in mind when planning or conducting the meeting

- Ideas for opening the meeting

- Discussion suggestions

- Ideas for concluding the meeting

- After-the-meeting follow-up suggestions

In cases where a topic requires more than one meeting, each session has its own opening, discussion, and conclusion ideas.

As noted earlier, these guidelines are examples of the three general types of class meetings: planning and decision making, check-in, and problem solving and consciousness raising. This section includes the following guidelines:

Planning and Decision-Making Meetings

Here We Are! (K–1)
Ways We Want Our Class to Be (K–2 and 2–6)
Class Name (K–6)
Back-to-School Night/Open House (K–6)
Substitutes (K–6)
Choosing to Learn (K–6)

Check-In Meetings

Is This the Way We Want to Be? (K–1 and 2–6)
What Did We Learn? (K–6)
How Did It Go with the Substitute? (K–6)

Problem-Solving and Consciousness-Raising Meetings

Problem Solving (K–6)
My Friends Won't Let Me Play (K–2)
Cliques (3–6)

These examples are just that—examples—not scripts or prescriptions or rote exercises. Like any practitioners' learning tool, they are *your* resource to be tried out, modified to suit your own and your class's makeup and needs, and perhaps used as helpful models as you begin planning class meetings on other topics.

That's a Plan!

PLANNING and decision-making meetings can help students establish ways they want to treat each other, activities they want to do together, and things they want to learn.

Here We Are!

GRADES K–1

Helping Children
Establish a Sense
of Well-Being
and Purpose

" I do unity builders a lot
during the first month
of school . . . For many
kindergartners, this is their
first group experience.
Then three or four weeks
into the year, we talk about
norms—but all the while
in the first weeks, we're
talking about why we come
to school and what we want
to learn."

$\mathcal{M}$ OST children hold great expectations
about school the first weeks of kindergarten and first grade, and for many these early
weeks are their first experience with learning in
a formal setting. Although many parents and
older family members may warn children to
"mind the teacher" and "be good," it is less
common for grown-ups to talk with them about
what the children hope for or might expect
from school.

This class meeting encourages children to think
of the school as "their own"—a community in
which they have a place, a stake, and a sense of
belonging—thereby building their motivation
to learn and to participate in the life of their
classroom.

Special Considerations • Part of establishing
children's sense of school as "their place" is to
familiarize them with the physical environment
and school routines. This is a big topic in itself;
don't be tempted to combine it with this meeting. Make a separate time for an introduction to
the "logistics" of the children's school community—location of bathrooms, where to find what,
and so on. Keep this "Here We Are!" meeting
focused on helping children establish a sense of
well-being about their place and participation in
school life.

The Class Meeting

Ideas for Opening the Meeting

■ **Explain "meetings."**

As this will probably be your students' first experience of a class meeting, begin by briefly welcoming them to the meeting and explaining that class meetings are a chance for them to talk about being in school. (Don't worry about ground rules at this point; introduce them gradually over several meetings.)

■ **Invite student talk about their hopes for the year.**

Ask students what they want to do in school this year. If students are reluctant to talk or can't seem to think of ideas, remind them of some of the activities they have already participated in, such as reading books, playing with classmates, and painting. On the other hand, if students have a lot of ideas to share, you might give them a few minutes to turn to a neighbor for a partner chat, and then have pairs share their ideas with the whole group.

■ **Record student ideas.**

As students share their ideas, write them on a large sheet of paper.

Discussion Suggestions

■ **Build discussion of each idea.**

Invite class discussion of the ideas as they are shared, encouraging children to ask questions about or embellish each other's ideas. Ask such questions as:

- Does anyone else have an idea like this?
- Does anyone have something else to say about this idea?
- Would anyone like to ask (Amika and Jack) a question about their idea?

■ **Let everyone contribute.**

Make sure that every child who has something to say gets to do so (especially as this is their first chance to experience class meetings as *their* forum). If the class is quite large and the situation permits, you might consider having initial meetings with half of the class at a time; this will allow time for everyone to speak without requiring anyone to sit still and listen for too long.

■ **Review the list and anticipate how the hopes it describes might be met.**

Review the list with the class, commenting on their interests and how these might play out in the year ahead. For example: "I see that many of us want to learn to read. We're going to start by reading many books together and writing stories."

Or, "A lot of you say you want to make new friends. Every day we will work and play together, so you will get to know everyone in our class."

■ **Add children's new ideas to the list.**

Encourage children to voice any questions or additions to the list that your comments might prompt.

Ideas for Concluding the Meeting

■ **Post the list, and ask students to keep thinking about it.**

After going over the list, tell students that you will leave it posted and that they can suggest things to add to it if other ideas occur to them.

■ **Synthesize what the ideas mean about the people in the class.**

Sum up what the list demonstrates. For example: everyone in the class has things they want to learn this year, the class is a group of people who want to learn, and each child—each learner—belongs to this community of learners.

■ **Invite students to reflect on the meeting.**

Give students a chance to talk about how the meeting went. Ask what they liked about the meeting and what they didn't like. Ask them what they might want to change the next time they have a meeting.

After the Meeting

The work you accomplished in this meeting can contribute to the ongoing life of the class and serves to introduce the next meeting.

■ **Our Community.** Leave the students' list posted, and add to it as students suggest. The list serves several purposes, not the least of which is that it graphically represents the students as a community, and you can regularly refer to it to develop their sense of membership in the community.

■ **Sharing the List at Home.** Make a copy of the list for each child to take home. In class, have students practice with a partner how they will explain the list to a parent or other adult at home.

■ **Next Meeting.** Follow this meeting with several check-in meetings in which children talk about "What Did We Learn?" (see page 90). Then move on to the "Ways We Want Our Class to Be" meeting (see page 53), in which students think about what they can *do* to make their classroom a place where they can feel good about school and learn well together.

aN important part of the school experience for young children is simply learning how to live with others. Having children participate in establishing norms for "ways we want our class to be" can contribute greatly to their understanding and sense of community. But because children in kindergarten and first grade have relatively little experience in negotiating the social world, they need many opportunities to have discussions, guided by adults, in which they can reflect on their own experiences and on how their behaviors affect other children in the class.

Class meetings offer a vehicle for such discussions and learning, and this meeting gets things started by helping children recognize the kinds of behaviors that make them feel good about school and about themselves. Note that the discussion goes from concrete examples to general principles, deepening children's understanding of such abstract concepts as kindness, fairness, and responsibility by helping them connect the things they *do* with the way they want to "be."

Special Considerations • Give children many opportunities to get to know one another and become acclimated to the school experience before holding a class meeting on norms. The "Getting-to-Know-You Activities" in Part One (see page 20) and the previous "Here We Are!" class meeting (see page 50) are recommended prerequisites to this meeting.

Likewise, keep in mind that young children need to have their understanding of these norms developed and reinforced throughout the year. You will want to hold regular meetings about the class norms—whether prompted by the general value of reflecting on them, a specific

Ways We Want Our Class to Be

GRADES K–2

Helping Children Establish Class Norms for Their Learning and Behavior

Be nice.

No name calling.

Play with people if they don't have anybody to play with.

Make friends.

Do not catch bees."

troublesome incident that needs to be addressed in these terms, or the introduction of a new norm or procedure. Always link these subsequent conversations with the students' original discussion and ideas about "ways we want our class to be."

Session One: Generating Ideas

Ideas for Opening the Meeting

■ **Explain the meeting purpose.**

Explain that the purpose of this meeting is to talk about ways we want our class to be—how we like to be treated and want to treat each other.

■ **Have students engage in a partner chat about how children treat each other at school.**

Invite students to describe times at school when they saw or experienced children doing something that made them feel good and times when didn't like what they saw or experienced. Get their thinking started by asking for a few examples, using questions such as the following:

• We want to talk about how we treat each other in school. Can anyone give me an example of something that made you feel good about being in school today? The way someone treated you, or something you saw someone do?

• Was there anything that didn't go so well? What happened?

Have students turn to a partner and tell each other examples of nice and not-so-nice things that happened. (Start them off with nice stories; you will probably need to remind them after a few minutes to talk about the second, not-so-nice topic.)

Discussion Suggestions

■ **Invite students to discuss concrete behaviors.**

Invite volunteers to tell about their examples of nice things that happened and things that made them feel bad. As students offer their examples, ask such questions as the following:

• Why did this make you feel good? Why didn't you feel good about this?

• Does anyone have another example like this one?

■ **Record the behaviors children relate.**

As children share their stories, record the events and behaviors on chart paper. Make two lists, one of the positive and one of the negative things described.

■ **Review the lists.**

When everyone has finished contributing to the two lists, read them aloud and check with students on each item, asking "Why is this the way we want to be (or don't want to be) in our class?"

■ **Post the lists for reference, and use in the next meeting.**

Ideas for Concluding the Meeting

■ **Preview the upcoming meeting.**

Let children know that they will use the lists later for another discussion about how they want their class to be, but that in the meantime they can try to keep the lists in mind and act in ways that make people feel good about school.

Session Two: What the Ideas Represent

Ideas for Opening the Meeting

■ **Review the "positive" list.**

Read aloud the "positive" list generated by students at the previous meeting, and briefly check with them to see if they want to add anything to the list.

■ **Introduce vocabulary.**

Introduce a few of the abstract words that describe the children's positive examples, such as *fair, kind,* and *responsible,* and the related antonyms, such as *unfair, unkind,* and *irresponsible,* that describe the negative examples.

■ **Categorize the examples.**

Characterize each item on the list for the children as an act of kindness, fairness, or responsibility—for example, "When someone walks you to the nurse's office, that person is being kind. And when you let someone have a turn on the swings, you're being fair." Explain that these are all ways we "take care"—of ourselves, of each other, of the classroom. If items fall into more than one category, acknowledge that—the point here isn't how accurately the behaviors are categorized, but that children consider the effect of their behavior on others and celebrate their own acts of kindness, fairness, and responsibility.

Discussion Suggestions

■ **Invite children to find other examples of kindness, fairness, or responsibility.**

Ask students to think of any other ways that people in the class can act kindly, fairly, and responsibly. Add these to the list of positive behaviors. (If necessary, help children relate these categories to situations that are especially likely to cause problems and call for considerate behavior—for example, lining up for recess, sharing the computer, cleaning up.)

■ **Relate kindness, fairness, and responsibility to children's goals for the year.**

Take a few minutes to review the list students made in the "Here We Are!" class meeting, regarding what they want to learn and do this year in school. Select some items from the list that lend themselves to this discussion of kindness, fairness, and responsibility, and point out those examples to the class. For instance, if students expressed eagerness to learn how to read, talk about how sharing books is a fair way to help everyone learn. Invite students to choose a goal and describe how kindness, fairness, or responsibility might be important.

■ **Ask partners to tell each other about one behavior they would like to work on.**

Have children turn to a partner and talk about one principle or behavior that they think is very important or that they would like to work on.

Ideas for Concluding the Meeting

■ **Have children make "Ways We Want Our Class to Be" drawings.**

Have each child draw or write a sign about a particular act of kindness, fairness, or responsibility that he or she would like everyone to remember. Explain that you will post these around the room to help everyone remember the way they want their class to be.

■ **Refer to the "negative" list as things the whole class will work on.**

Let children know that you haven't forgotten the "negative" list and that the class will work together to deal with items on that list. (You might address these in check-in or problem-solving class meetings, depending upon the nature and "size" of the problems students have included in the negative list.)

After the Meeting

■ **A Special Tour.** You may want to give children a day or two to complete their drawings or signs and then post them around the room. Conduct a "tour" of the drawings and signs so that children can see their classmates' work. Then invite students' general impressions of what these drawings say about the way they want their class to be. Reiterate that the drawings and signs will help everyone remember the important ways children want to treat each other, especially when difficulties arise.

WHEN students have no input into the "ways they want their class to be," class rules may seem as arbitrary as this rhyme governing the theft of pins and potatoes. But when students participate in the establishment of class rules and norms, they are naturally more committed to abiding by them and holding themselves accountable. Since the students are the ones who deliberated on the issues involved, the norms make sense to them, they believe in them, and they are invested in them. Essentially, they have told themselves how to behave, rather than being told how to behave— and they are more likely to listen to their own advice!

Session One: Generating Ideas

Ideas for Opening the Meeting

- **Explain the meeting purpose.**

  Explain that the purpose of this meeting is for the students to establish class norms for making their classroom a place where everyone feels safe, respected, cared for, and able to learn.

- **Have partners make idea lists of specific ways they want their class to be.**

  Use the Partner Idea List format (see suggestions for doing Partner Idea List on page 35) to have pairs of students brainstorm and discuss specific ways they want their class to be. Encourage students to think about their whole school day—how they like to be treated when they have something to say in a class discussion, during lunch and recess,

Ways We Want Our Class to Be

GRADES 2–6

Helping Children Establish Class Norms for Their Learning and Behavior

I t is a sin
To steal a pin;
It is a greater
To steal a potater.[1]

during quiet reading time, and so on. What will make the class a place where they feel comfortable, welcome, and ready to learn? Emphasize that the job right now is to be specific: if their partner says something general such as "be respectful," suggest that students ask for more detail — "What does that mean? What does that look like?"

■ **Have partners write or draw about their most important ideas.**

Ask partners to choose two or three ideas that are most important to both of them and write or draw each idea on a separate sentence strip or piece of paper.

■ **Write or draw about two or three ideas yourself.**

Save your examples for use in the second meeting.

Discussion Suggestions

■ **Have the class discuss the partners' chosen ideas.**

Ask the pairs of students to tell the rest of the class about the ideas that they agreed were important to them both. Invite class discussion of the ideas as they are shared, and encourage children to voice comments or questions as you go along. Ask such questions as the following:

- Does anyone have the same idea or a similar idea?
- Does anyone have a question or comment about this idea?
- Do you think it is always (never) a good (bad) idea to . . . ?
- Why is this important to you?

If an idea seems objectionable or controversial to other students, ask how it might be modified to be more acceptable to everybody.

Ideas for Concluding the Meeting

■ **Allow time for students to revise their work.**

If necessary, give partners additional time to revise or finalize their sentences or drawings.

■ **Preview the upcoming meeting.**

Explain that at the next meeting the class will categorize these ideas and come up with a class list of "Ways We Want Our Class to Be" and a set of class norms.

■ **Invite students to reflect on the meeting.**

Give students a chance to talk about how the meeting went. Ask them what they learned, what they liked and didn't like about the meeting, and whether they would do anything differently in their next meeting.

Session Two: Organizing Ideas

Before the Meeting

■ **Make and post signs for "fairness," "kindness and consideration," "responsibility," and "?."**

Post each sign over a different area of the chalkboard or blank wall space. Students will post their ideas under these signs later in the meeting. Leave masking tape near each sign.

Ideas for Opening the Meeting

■ **Introduce the concepts "fairness," "kindness and consideration," and "responsibility."**

Refer to the ideas partners wrote or drew about in the previous meeting, and introduce the values of fairness, kindness and consideration, and responsibility as ways to categorize those ideas about how students want their class to be. Assess students' understanding of the concepts, and if necessary address any glaring misunderstandings.

■ **Categorize your example ideas.**

Read one of your sentences or describe one of your pictures. Post it under one of the three value signs and explain why you choose that concept. Ask students to suggest a value category for your second idea.

■ **Invite students to categorize and post the ideas from their partnerships.**

Remind partners that the categorization requires their joint decision. Point out that if no category seems right, partners may choose the "?" location.

Discussion Suggestions

■ **Review the items in each category.**

With the class, go through the ideas posted in the three value categories. Encourage discussion of each categorization decision so that students will refine their understanding of the concepts. For example, ask questions such as the following:

• Why did you decide to put your idea in this category?

• Were there other categories you could have chosen as well?

• What does your idea have in common with other ideas in that category?

■ **Ask the class to suggest additional categories or examples as necessary.**

For the ideas in the "?" category, ask the class to create other categories to suit these items, such as "safety" or "pleasant environment."

If some norms have few examples, ask for additional ideas. For example:

- What are some other ways we can show fairness (kindness and consideration, responsibility)?

- Does anyone have other ideas about how to be kind and considerate to new students?

■ **Point out that the value categories are the class norms.**

Point out that students' own examples of how they want their class to be all demonstrate these norms. Emphasize that the norms apply to everyone in the classroom—not just students, but teachers and other adults as well. Ask students to consider what they would like best about their class if everyone acted with fairness, kindness and consideration, and responsibility (and any other categories that may have been created).

Ideas for Concluding the Meeting

■ **Discuss how to make the posted ideas into a list, poster, or class book.**

Ask students for ideas about organizing a list or poster for the class to display throughout the year, or discuss what a class book of their drawings could be like. Explain that the purpose of a list, poster, or book will be to help remind them of their own intentions to help others (such as volunteers or substitute teachers) and to serve as a reference for future discussions of norms or of situations to which the norms apply.

■ **Describe the class norms as a "living document."**

Encourage students to view this as *their* document: emphasize that students should feel free to suggest amendments or additions to the list of norms and examples throughout the year.

■ **Ask for volunteers to create the document.**

Provide support and materials for these students at a later time.

■ **Invite students to reflect on the meeting.**

Give students a chance to talk about how the meeting went. Ask them what they learned, what they liked and didn't like about the meeting, and whether they would do anything differently in their next meeting.

■ **Remind students that you will all talk about the norms often during the year.**
Explain that you will have other meetings to check in on how you all are doing with your norms or to discuss problems that may come up.

After the Meeting

Below are some ideas you could use to develop students' understanding of and commitment to the class norms. You might use one or two of these soon after the class meeting, or you could use them later in the year to review and reinforce the students' ideas about ways they want their class to be.

■ **If Someone Were**... Students can use this activity to further explore the meanings of the class norms. The "If Someone Were . . . " format asks children to define these values in a dramatic context—for instance, by acting out such statements as "If someone were fair, she would let everyone have a chance to give his or her ideas" or "If someone were kind, he would share his crayons with people who had forgotten theirs." Have students work in pairs to generate, rehearse, and dramatize their own "If someone were . . ." statements.

■ **Class Norm Posters.** Have students work individually or in pairs to create posters showing examples of the class norms.

■ **Is This the Way We Want to Be?** Use this check-in class meeting periodically during the year to remind yourselves of successes and ways to improve (see guideline on page 86). Or address particular problems that students may have in sticking to their norms with a problem-solving class meeting (see guideline on page 100).

■ **Sharing Norms at Home.** Have students each make a copy of the class norms to take home. In class, have students practice with a partner how they will explain the norms to a parent or other adult at home. Extend the activity by having students interview the adult about "Norms in Our Home" or "Norms Where I Work."

■ **Norms in Different Places.** Have students discuss how their class norms apply in the lunch room, on the playground, in sports, on the bus, etc.

■ **When We Work Together.** Before students work together in partnerships or small groups, ask them to predict ways their class norms might apply. Following the group work, ask them to reflect on successes or problems they had in their collaboration.

■ **Class Norm Rhymes.** Rhymes about behavioral norms, such as the one that opened this guideline, appear frequently in children's folklore. Recite a few from your own childhood, or read aloud the rhymes below (from Carl Withers's *A Rocket in My Pocket: The Rhymes and Chants of Young Americans*). Have students discuss how the rhymes fit, or don't fit, with their class norms. Then invite them to create their own rhymes about their class norms—establishing class norms may be serious, but it needn't be humorless!

> Me, myself, and I—
> We went to the kitchen and ate a pie.
> Then my mother she came in
> And chased us out with a rolling pin.

■

> Policeman, policeman, don't catch me!
> Catch that boy behind a tree.
> He took the money, I took none;
> Put him in the jailhouse, just for fun.

■

> Matthew, Mark, Luke, and John,
> Stole a pig and away they run;
> The pig got loose and they stole a goose,
> And all got thrown in the calaboose.

■

> Tit for tat,
> Butter for fat;
> If you kick my dog,
> I'll kick your cat.

■

> Mabel, Mabel, strong and able,
> Keep your elbows off the table,
> This is not a horse's stable.

■ ■

WHEN students choose a class name, they are building a sense of commonly held identity, which contributes to their feeling of unity as a class. In discussing and agreeing on a class name, students develop their consensus-building skills in a process that respects both diversity and unity among class members.

Special Considerations • This meeting should occur early in the year but not before students have a chance to get acquainted and some characteristics of the class begin to emerge (see pages 20–23 for Getting-to-Know-You activity suggestions). In order for a class name to be meaningful, and the process of finding one to be interesting, students need enough information about themselves as a group for the name to reflect the character of the class in some way.

Because this meeting occurs early in the year, students may be inexperienced or out of practice at building consensus with their peers. Make sure that students understand the process of building consensus; but even more important, make sure they understand the reasons for trying to achieve consensus. (See pages 36–41 for a discussion of consensus building.) Also note that because brainstorming and choosing the name could take some time, you may decide to schedule more than one meeting (possible stopping points are suggested in the text below).

Class Name

GRADES K–6

Helping Children Establish a Special Sense of Identity as a Community

"Blue Angels"

"Angel Territory"

"Bookers"

"Big Bad Bookers"

"Friendly Bookers"

"The High Fives"

"The Die Hards"

"The Try Hards"

The Class Meeting

Ideas for Opening the Meeting

■ **Explain the meeting purpose.**

Explain the purpose of the meeting, and discuss what it means to find a name that reflects characteristics of the class.

■ **Have the class offer examples of meaningful names.**

To get students thinking along these lines, give an example of a name or nickname that tells something about a person or animal (yourself, one of your pets, someone you know; or make one up). Ask students for their own examples: Do they have pets at home whose names describe a characteristic of the animal? Do they know people with (nonderogatory) nicknames that describe them?

Discussion Suggestions

■ **Have students work in pairs to generate ideas.**

Explain that first you want students to work in pairs to create Partner Idea Lists of potential class names and that then the whole class will work together to narrow down the options and agree on one choice. If necessary, review or explain how to create a Partner Idea List (see instructions on page 35). (Alternatively, use the Partner Idea List discussion questions below for a whole-class discussion, if that better suits the age or experience of your class.)

To help students think about class names that express how class members feel about their class, suggest that they discuss such questions as the following:

• What is special about our class?

• What do we do well together as a class?

• What things do we enjoy doing as a class?

• What do we like about the people in our class?

• What would we like others to know about our class?

• How would we like others to feel about our class?

• What goals do we have for our class?

• What words or names capture how we feel about our class and what we do well?

(Depending upon how engaged students are in this activity, the time it is taking, and their attention span, you may want to end here and save the class discussion for another meeting.)

■ **Have the class consider the possible class names.**

Invite partnerships to present their agreed-upon ideas to the whole group, and encourage them to explain the reasoning behind their choices. Invite the class to discuss each idea as it is presented, asking questions such as the following:

- Does anyone else have the same name or a similar name on their list?
- What does this name say about our class?
- What do we like about this name?
- What don't we like about it?
- How could we change this name to make it more acceptable to everybody?

Write each idea in its final form on the board, and then begin the process of reaching consensus about one name. (Again, you may decide to stop at this point and save the consensus-building discussion for another meeting.)

■ **Have the class choose a name by consensus.**

To build consensus, begin by asking students why it is important for all class members to agree on a name. If necessary, review the principles of consensus building, and help students see that there are ways to reach a decision other than by voting. (Pages 38–41 include various strategies for helping students narrow the choices and arrive at consensus.)

■ **In the event of gridlock . . .**

If students seem gridlocked, you might adjourn the meeting and start a subsequent session with one of the following approaches:

- Begin the meeting by inviting students to briefly state the reasons for their preferences, without rebuttal or comment from other students. Then make a fresh start at achieving consensus, building on these comments.
- Have students work in pairs to make lists of what they like about each of the remaining names under consideration, and then invite them to share their ideas with the whole group.
- Have students work in pairs to try and combine all or some of the remaining ideas, and then invite them to share their ideas with the whole group.
- Have partners reach consensus on one choice and present their decision to another pair; then have the groups of four reach consensus and present their decision to another group of four; and so on.

■ **Celebrate your choice!**

How about a class toast?

Ideas for Concluding the Meeting

■ **Invite students to reflect on the consensus-building process.**

Have a class discussion about what was good and what was difficult about reaching consensus. Ask students to discuss what they learned about building consensus and about holding productive discussions and what they think could be done differently the next time the class needs to reach agreement on an issue.

After the Meeting

Have students brainstorm and agree on how the class will formalize the class name and introduce it to the school community. For example, they might try one or more of the following ideas:

■ **Class Name Banner, Flag, or Mural.** Have individuals, partners, or small groups design banners or flags with the class name as a motif, and hang these in the classroom. Similarly, the whole class could collaborate on one large banner, flag, or mural inspired by the class name.

■ **Class Name Newsletter.** Have students publish a newsletter for their parents that incorporates the class name in the masthead. The first issue might be dedicated to the class name itself—the process by which it was chosen, interviews with students about why they think the name "works," pictures of a class seal or banner design, and so on.

■ **Class Name Song or Poem.** Have students use the class name as the title, refrain, or inspiration for a song or poem.

■ **Class Door Sign.** This can be as simple as a nameplate, or it can be embellished with illustrations, students' names, class "quotes," etc.

*t*HE purpose of this meeting is to get students involved in planning a Back-to-School Night or Open House that reflects the class's character. The process fosters class unity by giving students a chance to appreciate what they are accomplishing and doing well together. Having a voice in how to represent the class accomplishments deepens their investment in the classroom community.

Special Considerations • Younger children will have limited experience with such events and will probably need extra help identifying the considerations and tasks associated with putting together a Back-to-School Night or Open House.

Session One: Generating Ideas

Ideas for Opening the Meeting

■ **Explain the meeting purpose.**

Explain that this class meeting is for students to help you plan a Back-to-School Night/Open House that shows their families and other visitors what is special about the class.

■ **Describe the event.**

Explain to the class (or remind them of, if students have prior experience) the purpose of the event—whether it is to provide information about the year ahead, to give visitors to the classroom some experience of what has been going on, or both. The purpose of the event will help to define students' participation.

Back-to-School Night/ Open House

GRADES K–6

Involving Students in How to Present Their Class to Parents

For younger students, bring pictures, stories, or artifacts from past Back-to-School Nights/Open Houses to give children concrete ideas of what the event can be like. Encourage students to ask questions to learn more about such events.

Discussion Suggestions

■ **Have students imagine being a visitor to their classroom.**

Ask students to imagine someone visiting their classroom for the first time: What would that person learn by looking around the room? Then encourage them to think about what they would *like* visitors to learn about their classroom community. If their parents, or grandparents, or siblings came to the classroom, what would they like them to know about the class? How would they like them to feel? How could this be accomplished? For example, use such questions as the following to stimulate their thinking and discussion:

• What do we want visitors to know about our class?
  How is our class special?
  What do we like about our class?

• What do we want visitors to know about what we are learning? How can we show them this?
  What have we done so far?
  What are some of our plans?

• What do we want visitors to know about how we work together? How can we show them this?

• What do we want visitors to know about how we play together? How can we show them this?

• How can we help visitors feel "at home" in our classroom?
  What can I (the teacher) do to help visitors feel at home?
  What can you (the students) do to make visitors feel at home?

• Some people might not be able to attend our Back-to-School Night/Open House. What can we do afterward to share with them what happened at the event?

■ **Record students' ideas.**

On chart paper, record students' ideas as you go along, perhaps in the form of a mind map or other graphic representation that helps students group their ideas according to the different kinds of goals of the event. For example, to help visitors learn about what the class is learning, students might suggest setting up displays, producing written materials, and performing dramatic role-plays; to help visitors feel welcome and at home they might suggest cleaning the classroom, making a guest book, having "docents" provide tours of the classroom, serving refreshments, and so on.

■ **Review the ideas.**

Review the students' ideas with the class and add anything else that comes up. If students have difficulty generating ideas for their Back-to-School Night or Open House activities, you might describe one or more of the following to spark their thinking:

- Produce a newsletter for guests who will be visiting the classroom. This gives students an opportunity to tell family members and friends about their class; it can also be sent home to parents or grandparents who were unable to attend the event.

- Present visitors with information on the class name and how and why it was chosen.

- Present visitors with information about the class norms and how these norms were arrived at.

- Serve refreshments.

- Create a guest book for visitors to the classroom. Besides signing it, guests can fill in other information that students may wish to gather (such as special interests or talents guests might share with the class sometime, guests' reactions to their classroom visit, what they learned from the visit, and so on).

Ideas for Concluding the Meeting

■ **Preview the upcoming meeting.**

Tell students that they will be meeting again to do more planning, and ask them in the meantime to think about the ideas and what the class will need to do to prepare for Back-to-School Night/Open House.

■ **Post the list of ideas.**

Leave the ideas posted until the next meeting.

■ **Invite students to reflect on the meeting.**

Give students a chance to talk about how the meeting went. Ask them what they learned, what they liked and didn't like about the meeting, and whether they would do anything differently in their next meeting.

Session Two: Logistics

Ideas for Opening the Meeting

■ **Explain the meeting purpose.**

Refer to the list of ideas generated in the previous session, and explain that you want students' help in figuring out which of these things they will be able to do and how to get them done.

Discussion Suggestions

■ **Help students establish criteria for choosing which ideas to pursue.**

If students have suggested more ideas than are practical to pursue, or ideas that may be impossible to complete, help them establish criteria that will refine their list. For example, get their thinking started by comparing how much time is available for working on their ideas and how many ideas they have suggested. Get them thinking about how many people, what kind of supplies, what kind of skills, etc., will be needed for each idea (see information about applying objective criteria on page 40).

■ **Narrow the list.**

Help students apply objective criteria as they finalize the list.

■ **Have students plan the implementation of each idea.**

Depending upon the age and experience of your students, as well as the number and range of ideas on their list, have students pair up, break into small groups, or remain in the whole-class group to discuss and plan the logistics that each idea entails.

For example, if the class has generated a lot of ideas, small groups could each take on one idea and outline the tasks and materials involved; if the class has just one plan in mind, pairs could each discuss that prospect and then share their ideas with the whole group; and so on. Younger students, however, might not have enough experience and information to think through the plans and tasks independently, so they would probably fare better in a whole-class discussion.

■ **Finalize the list and logistics.**

With the students, finalize the list and plans as necessary. For example, after delineating all the tasks involved in an idea, students may realize that the idea is simply too demanding and needs revision; or, if all students discussed one plan, they may need help to connect and combine their ideas in order to reach consensus on how to proceed, and so on. Help students "fill in the blanks" as to how the tasks are to be accomplished (for example, dividing some responsibilities among partners or small groups, pointing out logistical details, and so on).

Ideas for Concluding the Meeting

■ **Review responsibilities.**

Be sure students understand their group or individual responsibilities.

■ **Help students establish a timeline.**

With the class, establish a timeline for accomplishing the Back-to-School Night/ Open House activities and associated tasks.

■ **Invite students to reflect on the meeting.**

Give students a chance to talk about how the meeting went. Ask them what they learned, what they liked and didn't like about the meeting, and whether they would do anything differently in their next meeting.

After the Meeting

■ **Make yourself available to students, but not indispensable.**

■ **Periodically have students evaluate their progress and processes.**

After the Event

■ **Assess the Event and Student Efforts.** Have students report on visitors' responses (as written in the guest book, observed firsthand, and reported at home) to their efforts. Discuss the overall impact of the event.

■ **Send the Newsletter.** Send home copies of the class newsletter for those parents or grandparents who were unable to attend the event.

■ **Thank Contributors.** Have students write thank-you notes to parents or merchants who donated time, refreshments, or supplies.

■ **Invite a Buddy Class.** Have students share their efforts with a buddy class, explaining what they want visitors to know about their class.

■ **Use the Guest Book Information.** In addition to using guest book information to assess the event, invite guests to return to the classroom in whatever capacities they have indicated an interest.

Substitutes

GRADES K–6

Helping Students Plan and Take Perspective

"During a class meeting we talked about how we would feel if we were a substitute. Kids came up with things like, 'nervous' and 'stupid because you don't know everybody's name.' I asked them why they thought those things, and then we discussed what we could do to make the substitute feel comfortable . . . That really worked well. The substitute that the class later had said she had never been with such an attentive group of children."

WHEN the teacher is away, things can be difficult for both the students and the substitute teacher. This class meeting gives students a chance both to express their concerns about substitutes and to think about the feelings a substitute may have when in an unfamiliar classroom. Equipped with these awarenesses, students can help plan ahead for days when they will have a substitute teacher—and by giving students the initiative and a measure of control over the situation, you help make the experience of having a substitute more positive for everyone.

Special Considerations • Have this meeting early in the year, before you need to bring in a substitute. And, if possible, review the meeting conclusions immediately before a substitute's arrival. Plan a follow-up meeting for after the class has had a substitute, so that students can assess the success of the plan they developed (see "How Did It Go with the Substitute?" guideline on page 94).

Kindergarten teachers will want to keep in mind that young children may need help imagining what it means to have a substitute in the classroom. Spend extra time at the beginning of the meeting describing substitute teaching and what it involves.

The Class Meeting

Ideas for Opening the Meeting

■ **Explain the meeting purpose.**

Tell students that they will be planning for a substitute so that everyone will have a positive experience—themselves as well as the substitute.

■ **Engage students' experience of substitutes.**

No matter what the age range of your students, an enjoyable way to open this meeting would be to read Chapter 4, "The Substitute," from Beverly Cleary's *Ramona the Pest* (Ramona is in kindergarten in this book). For upper-grade students, follow the reading by having them talk with a partner about how their feelings and thinking about substitutes have changed since they were Ramona's age. For younger students, have the whole class or partners create a Venn diagram comparing their own feelings about substitutes with Ramona's. (The chapter stands on its own, but you may want to read the book from the beginning and hold the meeting to coincide with reading this chapter.)

For a more streamlined opening, have partners tell each other about a memorable experience they have had with substitute teachers or stories they have heard from older siblings or friends.

Discussion Suggestions

■ **Have students imagine their reactions to having a substitute.**

Begin by asking students to close their eyes and imagine coming into the classroom one morning to find a substitute teacher in your place. Ask such questions as the following to help children express how they might feel about this new situation:

- How did you feel when you imagined having a new teacher in our classroom? Why did you feel that way?

- How might school be different for you with a substitute in the classroom?
  What might be hard about having a substitute?
  What might be fun about having a substitute?

- What can we do to make it easier for you when we have a substitute? How would that help?
  What would you like the substitute to know about you?
  What would you like the substitute to know about the class?
  What would you like the substitute to know about how we work?
  What other things would you like the substitute to know about?

■ **Record students' ideas on a mind map or list.**

As the conversation proceeds, draw out students' thinking by asking them to elaborate, clarify, or give examples; record their ideas.

■ **Have students imagine being a substitute.**

Once students have had ample opportunity to express what they would like from the experience of having a substitute, ask them to close their eyes again and this time imagine *being* the substitute. Remind students that when the substitute enters the classroom and sees all the children, he or she won't know their names, where anything is, what the regular teacher usually does with the class, and so on. Ask such questions as the following to encourage their perspective taking:

• How did it feel to be the substitute walking into the classroom? Why did it feel that way?

• What do you think would be hardest about being the substitute? Why?

• What can we do to make things easier for a substitute teacher?
  What would a substitute need to know about you (the students)?
  What would a substitute need to know about the room?
  What would a substitute need to know about the school?
  What would a substitute need to know about how we work?
  What other things would be useful for the substitute to know?

■ **Record students' ideas.**

■ **Review the mind maps or lists.**

Review both sets of student ideas, and ask if students have any other issues about substitutes to bring up or any other suggestions about how to help the class and the substitute teacher.

■ **Have students choose some concrete ways to help the substitute.**

If necessary, introduce some of the following possibilities:

• Plan, write, and illustrate a *Substitute's Handbook.*

• Make name tags to wear when substitutes or other visitors come to the classroom.

• Create a seating chart illustrated with self-portraits or photographs of class members.

• Draw a map of the classroom with labels indicating where things are.

• Write a daily or weekly schedule listing important events such as recess, lunch, library, and dismissal times.

• Create a Substitute's Assistant rotating position, and define that person's duties.

• Create a Visitors' (which includes substitutes) Library that houses books and other materials created by and about the class (for example, about class norms).

Ideas for Concluding the Meeting

- **Help students plan the implementation of the chosen ideas.**

  Establish a timeline with students and set aside time for them to work individually, in pairs, or in small groups to implement these ideas.

- **Invite students to reflect on the meeting.**

  Give students a chance to talk about how the meeting went. Ask them what they learned, what they liked or didn't like about the meeting, and whether they would do anything differently in their next meeting.

After the Meeting

Use one or more of the ideas below to extend students' thinking about this topic.

- **Story Review.** If you opened the meeting by having partners tell each other stories about experiences with substitute teachers, ask students to turn to the same partner and talk about those stories again. Given their fresh insights and ideas from the class meeting, how might their stories have been different? What might students have done differently? Do they have a different "take" on their own or the substitute's part in the story?

- **Partner Biographies.** This activity builds students' sense of community, as well as their written and oral communication skills—and it also results in an addition to the Visitors' Library. Have students work in pairs to interview each other and write short biographies of their partners, including the subject's name, a few interesting personal facts, something he or she does particularly well or especially enjoys doing, and a drawing or photo of the student. The biographies could either be bound together into a class book, or they could be collected on file cards displaying the interview information on one side and the portrait on the other.

- **Substitute Guest Speaker.** Invite a substitute teacher to visit the classroom to talk about his or her experiences as a substitute (students might enjoy preparing interview questions for the speaker). Also give students an opportunity to share their feelings about substitutes with the speaker.

- **Substitute Reception.** Have the class plan an informal class or schoolwide reception for substitute teachers, in recognition of their contributions to the school. Holding this reception soon after the beginning of the year will introduce substitutes, teachers, and students to one another and welcome the substitutes into the school community.

Choosing to Learn

GRADES K–6

Engaging Students' Curiosity about Learning Topics

"What does your group want to study?"

"Water."

"*Nieve* (snow)."

"Sounds."

"Fire."

"Where does the universe end?"

CHILDREN are intrinsically motivated to learn. As educators, our goal (and challenge!) is to make their curiosity about the world our ally, to tap that motivation and make teaching and learning mutually rewarding. One way to accomplish this is to give students a role in choosing topics to study—topics that spark their interest and prompt them to think about significant ideas. This class meeting invites students to choose a topic for in-depth study and can be used in any subject area. For example, in science students might choose among studying the solar system, geology, or oceanography; in studying state history students might choose to focus on Native Americans, settlers, regional culture, or achieving statehood; and in reading students might choose among several books, each representing a different theme.

Special Considerations • It is not always necessary or even desirable for the whole class to study the same topic—this class meeting can also be used to identify and discuss different options from which small groups, partners, or individuals may choose. For example, rather than having the whole class study one artist, it may be more significant to have different students or groups specialize in different artists and then compare and contrast what they have learned. Similarly, partnerships might choose from several books that share a common theme, such as friendship or courage, and then discuss their reading with students who chose a different book with that theme.

The Class Meeting

Please note: For the sake of clarity, the meeting outlined below assumes that students are choosing one topic to be studied by the whole class.

Ideas for Opening the Meeting

■ **Explain the meeting purpose.**

Explain that students will be selecting a topic the class will study in depth. Assure them that the process will not be one of voting, but of investigating and reaching consensus.

■ **Introduce the possible topics.**

Tailor the amount of introduction and investigation of topics to their importance and the commitment required. Begin by giving students the flavor of each topic (limit the number of topics to keep the process manageable) by reading interesting excerpts from books or magazines, showing video clips, displaying artifacts, and the like. For example, you could introduce possible book choices by reading short, enticing passages from each (choosing passages that avoid giving away the story), you could show the art of several artists that students might study, you could create posters about the highlights of an historical period being considered, and so on. Similarly, you might have partners skim through textbook chapters covering possible topics, encouraging them to look at pictures and read captions to get a general sense of each topic.

■ **Give students time to talk together.**

After students have been exposed to all the possible topics, have them pair up to discuss their preferences, and then have each partnership share ideas with another partnership. In this way, students will be able to consider a variety of perspectives before the whole-class discussion. Also remind students that the topic will be decided by consensus, so that even if the final choice is not everyone's first preference, it will be one that everyone finds interesting and worthwhile in some way.

Discussion Suggestions

■ **Open the discussion of topics.**

Invite students to share with the class their ideas and opinions about the topics (you might deal with one topic at a time or open the floor for general discussion of the topics in no particular order). Ask such questions as:

• Which of these topics interests you most, and why?

• What are your thoughts and feelings about this topic?

• What are some reasons for learning more about this topic?

Follow up on students' responses by asking for clarification and elaboration, when appropriate or necessary, and by inviting students to respond to each other.

■ **Record students' ideas.**

For each topic, make a list recording students' reasons for wanting to study it.

You might want to stop after the general discussion of topics (depending on time and the breadth of opinion that needs to be tackled) and hold a second session for reaching consensus, perhaps allowing more time for investigation first.

Ideas for Concluding the Meeting

■ **Build consensus about a topic of study.**

Begin moving the class toward consensus by summarizing responses, using such statements as, "Most of the interest seems to be in —— and ——. Does that seem accurate?" As the field narrows, give students a chance to comment on the remaining options, to suggest ways to compromise or combine ideas, and so on. Continue until consensus has been reached. (See pages 36–41 for information on building consensus.)

■ **Celebrate the chosen topic.**

With an appropriate toast, song, or other gesture, celebrate the beginning of your study topic. (See also the "Launch" follow-up suggestion below.)

■ **Invite students to reflect on the meeting.**

Give students a chance to talk about how the meeting went. Ask them what they liked or didn't like about the meeting and the process of reaching consensus.

After the Meeting

Choosing a topic is a first step in learning. Now immerse students in the topic, using activities such as those suggested below, and continue to solicit student input (both formally and informally) to guide your teaching on the topic.

■ **Launch.** Once students have chosen the topic, launch the study with a celebration, preferably something consistent with the selected topic (for example, a kite-flying party to launch a weather study). To further engage students and enhance their sense of "ownership" of the topic, you might recruit a student committee to plan the celebration.

- **Brainstorm: What We Know.** Have partners or small groups brainstorm everything students know—or think they know—about the topic. As students learn more, periodically have them return to these lists and note whether their ideas were true, not true, or whether they still need additional information.

- **Brainstorm: What We Want to Know.** Have students brainstorm a list of questions they have about the topic. Encourage students to pose their questions in the form of "I wonder . . . " or "I want to learn more about . . . " Use the questions to guide the inquiry.

- **Check-In Class Meeting.** At the end of the study, hold a class meeting to help students reflect on what they have learned. (For example, see the "What Did We Learn?" class meeting guideline on page 90; although it outlines a brief check-in meeting, it also offers "After the Meeting" suggestions for more extensive reflection.)

How Are We Doing?

CHECK-IN meetings let students reflect on how they're treating each other, what they're learning, and how well they're meeting their goals.

Is This the Way We Want to Be?

GRADES K–1

Helping Children Meet Their Goals

*e*VEN very young children have a sense of what is right and can express strong opinions about what is just and fair—yet they often excuse themselves from the very norms they hold so dear for others. This class meeting helps students connect class norms developed at the beginning of the year (in the "Ways We Want Our Class to Be" meeting) to everyday behavior, when doing the right thing sometimes conflicts with doing the attractive or popular thing. Held periodically throughout the year, this class meeting will deepen students' understanding of norms such as kindness, fairness, honesty, and responsibility—and will help them align their behavior with their ideals.

Session One: Our Progress

Ideas for Opening the Meeting

- **Explain the meeting purpose.**

  Explain that in this meeting children will check to see what things they are doing that make their class a good place to be. (Tell students that they will talk about ways to improve their class in a later meeting.)

- **Remind students of their earlier norm-setting meeting.**

  Draw students' attention to the class norms that they agreed to in their "Ways We Want Our Class to Be" meeting earlier in the year, and invite volunteers to read or recall what the class decided then.

Discussion Suggestions

■ **Describe a positive example or two that you have observed.**

Talk about successes by pointing out the many ways that students are being kind, fair, and responsible (or substitute wording from the class norms or other classroom vocabulary). Give a concrete example of a norm in action—something you observed recently that made the class a place where people felt cared for, safe, respected, and able to learn. Describe, for example, a recent situation when two children who had finished cleaning up the library station began helping the children who were cleaning up the painting station.

■ **Ask students to describe positive examples from their experience.**

Ask students for examples of ways they have seen children treat each other well: What are people doing that makes our class a place we want to be? Ask children to describe in detail something they saw that they liked.

Ideas for Concluding the Meeting

■ **Summarize what the children's examples show about their class.**

Let students know, for example, that if there were several stories about sharing materials, the class is doing a good job of being fair; if students have learned to help each other clean up, they are doing a good job of being responsible; and so forth.

■ **Take pleasure in the class's successes.**

Celebrate the way the children have created a caring community, perhaps by singing a song, such as "The More We Are Together, the Happier We'll Be."

Session Two: Ways to Improve

Ideas for Opening the Meeting

■ **Explain the meeting purpose.**

Remind students of the successes they celebrated in the previous meeting, and then explain that during this session you want everyone to think about what they could still work on to make their class the way they want it to be.

Discussion Suggestions

■ **Ask students to describe recent negative examples.**

Invite students to describe a time during the day (or week) when people were treated in ways that made them feel bad. Ask them to describe in detail what they saw that they didn't like (see "Establishing Ground Rules" on page 23 for suggestions on avoiding a "shaming" environment in such discussions).

■ **Categorize students' examples.**

Categorize the described problems according to the class norms. For example, if students reported that it's hard to get to play in the block corner, get enough details to determine whether this is a problem of not taking turns (unfairness) or whether it's a problem of keeping certain people out (unkindness).

Review the categories and summarize the norms that people are concerned about.

■ **Prioritize the problems.**

From among all the examples, help the class choose two or three that are "most important" to talk about (perhaps because they affect the most people, are the most egregious, or represent a manageable first step).

■ **Discuss the "most important" problems.**

Have the class discuss the chosen problems one at a time, using such questions as:

• Why is this a problem?

• Why do you think this happens?

• What could we do about this problem?

Throughout, help children remain focused on the problem, not the perpetrators, and on solutions, not punishment. (If an issue seems quite imposing or generates a lot of discussion, you may decide to hold a full-fledged problem-solving meeting to address it; see the "Problem Solving" class meeting guideline on page 100.)

Ideas for Concluding the Meeting

■ **Help students reflect on what they learned.**

Bring students back to the goal of making the class a place where everyone wants to be. Help students reflect on the discussion by asking general questions, such as:

• What have we learned from this discussion?

• What could we do better to make this class a happy and safe place for everyone?

• Can we add anything to our ideas about ways we want our class to be?

Don't worry about developing a plan of action or achieving consensus—simply raising awareness of the issues is achievement enough for this meeting. As students identify and discuss their concerns, they deepen their understanding of the relationship between class norms and everyday behavior, renew their commitment to the norms, and strengthen their sense of the caring classroom community.

After the Meeting

The most obvious follow-up to this meeting is another meeting of the same type. As mentioned above, this check-in meeting should be held periodically throughout the school year. You might also want to use the activities suggested below to help students reflect on the discussion and on the class goals.

- **The Problem and Me.** Have students employ their emerging literacy skills in writing about an experience they had that relates to a problem discussed in the class meeting (or have them draw about it).

- **Problem Literature.** Read aloud a book about a problem the class has discussed, and help students make connections between the story and their own experience.

- **Role-Play.** Invite volunteers to role-play a brief scenario related to the problem discussed by the class. Present the players with a situation (for example, two children are playing with all the blocks and another child wants to play), and have them enact a solution. Ask the class what they think of the actors' solution: Do they think it worked? Did it make everybody feel good? What else might they have done to make everybody happy?

- **Partner-Play.** Have students work with partners to role-play solutions to a problem between two students. (Remind partners that their first job will be to decide who will play whom.) Invite volunteers to perform their role-play for the class, to give students a chance to see that there are different solutions to the same problem.

- **What Can I Do?** Ask students to write or draw about what they might do to fulfill the class norm discussed in the meeting or about what they personally intend to do to help solve the problem that was discussed.

Is This the Way We Want to Be?

GRADES 2–6

Helping Children Meet Their Goals

*A*T THE beginning of the school year, in the "Ways We Want Our Class to Be" meeting, students created a list of norms for making their classroom a community where everyone feels safe, respected, cared for, and able to learn. Establishing class norms was just the first step, however. The real challenge for students and teachers comes in applying abstract norms, such as kindness, fairness, consideration, and responsibility, to everyday situations—when doing the right thing sometimes conflicts with doing the popular or easy thing. Held regularly throughout the year, this "check-in" class meeting will help students reflect on their goals for ways they want their class to be, identify areas that need more work, and more closely align their actions with their ideals.

Session One: Status Report

Ideas for Opening the Meeting

- **Explain the meeting purpose.**

   Remind students of how they created their list of class norms at the beginning of the year, and explain that the purpose of the meeting is to review the class norms and check in on how they are being fulfilled and what might need work.

- **Have partners list achievements and problems.**

   After a volunteer reads aloud the posted list of class norms, ask students to discuss with a partner how they think the class is doing at meeting their norms. Ask partners to create a list of what is working well, and another list of what is not working. Encourage them to be specific about types of successes and problems. For example, "People push to get to the equipment locker at recess to grab the balls and then think they 'own' them" is more specific and useful than "We are having trouble sharing sports equipment," which, in turn, is more specific and useful than "We are not being fair at recess." Also encourage students to identify *behaviors*, not the individuals associated with them—this is a conversation about what everyone needs to do to maintain class norms, not about how one or two people need to improve their behavior.

Discussion Suggestions

■ **Have partners share their lists of successes.**

Devote this session's discussion to successes. Invite partners to share one or two items from their lists of what is going well, and write these on the board or on chart paper. Help students make connections between their own and other students' ideas by asking such questions as the following:

• Does anyone have an example that is similar to this?

• Would anyone like to add to this idea?

Group the ideas to highlight major themes that emerge, or invite students to draw their own conclusions by asking open-ended questions, such as the following:

• What do you notice?

• What are some things people seem to agree on?

Ideas for Concluding the Meeting

■ **Review and summarize the class list.**

End the meeting on a positive note: review the class list of what is going well and how these examples contribute to everyone's (including your own) sense of classroom community.

■ **Invite students to reflect on the meeting.**

Ask students what they learned and what they liked and didn't like about the meeting.

■ **Preview the upcoming meeting.**

Let students know that at the next session they will have a chance to focus on things that aren't going quite so well.

Session Two: Ways to Improve

Ideas for Opening the Meeting

■ **Explain the meeting purpose.**

Remind students of the successes they acknowledged in the previous meeting, and then explain that during this session you want everyone to think about what they could work on to better meet some of the class norms.

■ **Ask partners to review their "needs improvement" list.**

Give partners a few minutes to review the list they made during the last session of what doesn't seem to be working well; encourage them to add any new ideas.

Discussion Suggestions

■ **Record partners' ideas about what needs to improve.**

Invite partners to share one or two items from their lists of what they think isn't going well, and write their responses on the board or on chart paper.

■ **Encourage students to suggest groupings and themes.**

Help students see the relationships between items. For example, leaving someone out of a game and not letting someone sit with your group at lunch are both examples of excluding, and both violate a class norm of "acting with kindness and consideration."

■ **Have students prioritize their concerns.**

Have students agree on four or five "most important" topics to discuss now.

■ **Address one topic at a time.**

Focus on one topic at a time, and have students discuss how they might address it (don't be surprised if you only have time for one or two topics). Draw out students' thinking by asking them to elaborate, clarify, or give examples; also help them make connections between their own and other students' ideas.

Throughout, help students remain focused on the problem, not the perpetrators, and on solutions, not punishment. (If an issue seems quite imposing or generates a lot of discussion, you may decide to hold a full-fledged problem-solving meeting to address it; see the "Problem Solving" class meeting guideline on page 100.)

Ideas for Concluding the Meeting

■ **Help students reflect on what they learned.**

Bring the class back to the goal of making the class a place where everyone wants to be. Help students reflect on the discussion by asking a general question, such as:

• What have we learned from this discussion?

• What does this mean for us?

• Should we add anything to our list of ways we want our class to be?

Don't worry about developing a plan of action or achieving consensus—increasing awareness of problems and their impact on classmates should contribute to students' deeper commitment to classroom norms and sense of community.

After the Meeting

The most obvious follow-up to this meeting is another one like it. As stated above, this check-in meeting should be held periodically throughout the school year. You might also want to use the activities suggested below to extend the learning that occurred in the class meeting and to promote students' personal connection and commitment to the class norms.

■ **Personal Connection.** Have students write or draw about a personal experience related to one of the problems or solutions discussed during the meeting.

■ **Class Norms Revisions.** Have partners discuss whether any revisions should be made to the class norms, and hold another class meeting to discuss proposed changes.

■ **Problem Literature.** Read aloud a book about a problem the class has discussed, and help students make connections between the story and their own experience. Consider using picture books—their simplicity can be a great catalyst for discussion of important ideas, even with older students.

■ **The Moral of the Story.** Introduce students to stories that have a "moral," such as Arnold Lobel's *Fables*. Then, as a class, brainstorm a list of morals suggested by the "Is This the Way We Want to Be?" class meeting (both sessions). Be prepared to offer a few ideas of your own to get things going (for example, "Words *can* hurt"). Have partners or small groups write stories illustrating a moral from the class list.

■ **The Moral of the Skit.** Have students perform their moral stories for the class.

■ **What Can *I* Do?** Ask students to write or draw about what they might do to fulfill the class norm discussed in the meeting or about what they personally intend to do to help solve the problem discussed in the class meeting.

What Did We Learn?

GRADES K–6

Reinforcing Children's Feeling of Being in a Learning Community

"We learned about tens. Ten. Twenty. Thirty. Forty."

"We went to the library."

"We learned about penguins."

"Penguins lay eggs."

"The mama keeps them warm until the daddy comes back from catching fishes."

"They protect their babies from other animals."

"The little penguins get bigger and take care of themselves."

CHILDREN are frequently asked, "What did you learn in school today?"—to which they just as frequently shrug, "Nothing." This check-in class meeting, if held regularly, can help children appreciate and articulate what they learn in class. Besides recognizing their subject-matter learning, children will begin to recognize that they are learning to think things through, solve problems, work with others, make thoughtful choices, see things from different points of view, and be fair, kind, and responsible people. Children's ability to see themselves as learners is important to their confidence and progress as learners, and their ability to tell their families about what they have learned helps foster positive home-school relationships.

Special Considerations • This class meeting is useful at the close of the day, at the end of the week, or at the completion of a unit of study. Limit daily or weekly meetings to ten to fifteen minutes, and don't attempt a systematic review of everything the students did—just help them identify, discuss, and celebrate a few highlights in a leisurely manner. If you are using the meeting at the completion of a unit of study, students may enjoy being more comprehensive (see the "After the Meeting" suggestions).

The Class Meeting

Please note: For the sake of clarity, the description below assumes that these meetings are held daily.

Ideas for Opening the Meeting

■ **Explain the meeting purpose only if this kind of meeting is not yet institutionalized in your classroom.**

Talk with students about why your class will be having these meetings.

■ **Help students "warm up" their thinking.**

Choose one of the following suggestions for opening the meeting:

* Have partners interview each other about their day, perhaps focusing their conversations on a specific topic, such as "Something I learned today that was hard" or "The most surprising thing I learned" or the like. As students become more practiced and accustomed to these check-in meetings, give them increasing responsibility for the direction of the interviews.

* Have partners create Partner Idea Lists (see page 35) of what they have learned, starring the items that they have both learned (or enjoyed learning or found most challenging or the like). In this way, their lists will reflect both their common and individual learning and perspectives.

* Have students reflect on the day's learning by writing or drawing in a journal.

Discussion Suggestions

■ **Open the discussion of students' reflections about their day.**

Invite volunteers to share some of what they learned. Use questions such as the following to generate discussion, or your own questions tailored to the day's events, and use clarifying and follow-up questions to help students connect and build on each other's comments.

* Who would like to tell something they learned today?
  What did the class learn together?
  Did anyone learn something especially for himself or herself?

* How do you feel about the things you learned?
  What was hard about learning those things? Why?
  What was easy to learn? Why?
  What was fun/exciting/surprising about learning these things? Why?

- What did you learn about other people today?
- What did you learn about yourself today?
- What did you learn about working with other people today?
- What would you like to tell someone at home about what you learned today?

■ **Record students' ideas.**

Let this be a quick list to post in the classroom and/or notes for a class newsletter to be written later and sent home.

Ideas for Concluding the Meeting

■ **Add final observations.**

Ask students for any additional observations about the day or the discussion, and perhaps point out any efforts or accomplishments that you have observed. At times you might also want to suggest a simple activity to connect their observations to future activities, such as asking students to identify something they would like to learn more about the next day or add to a class Learning Encyclopedia (see below).

■ **Give students time to reflect on what they will report at home.**

Ask students to rehearse silently or to a partner what they will tell about their day to someone at home.

After the Meeting

Occasionally you may wish to supplement the meeting, or hold a more elaborate class meeting, by using one of the suggestions below.

■ **C is for Curious.** Younger children might enjoy this variation on the discussion: choose an appropriate page or two from Woodleigh Hubbard's *C is for Curious: An ABC of Feelings* (in which zany animals portray an alphabet of feelings), and discuss things that happened in school that day that evoked the illustrated feelings.

■ **A Week in the Life.** Ask students to draw pictures of themselves engaged in their favorite (most challenging, most interesting, etc.) learning activity of the week. Have them cut out and assemble their pictures on butcher paper or on a bulletin board to create a mural entitled "A Week in the Life of (class name)." Use the mural as a starting point for the class meeting, asking such questions as "Who wants to tell us about his or her drawing?" and "Who else showed this activity in the mural?"

- **Learning Encyclopedia.** Have students create an encyclopedia or file of significant things they learn throughout the year, and invite students to add to it whenever they learn something interesting or important to them. Entries need not be restricted to facts but can also include important understandings of all kinds. This record provides an opportunity for students to share their knowledge and find out who has similar interests.

- **Learning Newsletter.** Have students collect their learning experiences in writing for a weekly newsletter to send home.

- **Learning Journal.** Have students keep a journal in which they reflect on their learning. As suggested above, journal writing (or drawing) can be used to open the check-in meeting and prime the discussion; it could also be used to wrap up or alternate with the class meeting.

- **Learning More.** Reflecting on their learning can inspire students to learn more. To encourage this inclination, post a list where students can jot down ideas or subjects they would like to pursue either on their own or with the class.

- **Class History.** At the end of each week, have students list the memorable activities of the week—things they learned, places they visited, activities they did, people they met, and so on. Have a weekly scribe draw and/or write (or dictate) about these things for the class history book. Periodically review the class history with the students, and use the book at the end of the year to bring back memories and help them realize how much they have done. (This is particularly useful for young children to develop their sense of time and history and to underscore how valuable graphic and written records are.)

How Did It Go with the Substitute?

GRADES K–6

Helping Students Evaluate Their Planning

Poor Substitute

Gretchen has taken Freddy's
    chair,
Andrew's desk has no one
    there.

Sally was fighting for
    Tommy's space,
She won the battle and
    took his place.

Daryl is working at Jennie's
    desk,
And Joe just finished Maria's
    test.

Substitute teacher, you'd
    better beware,
Alicia just plopped in the
    teacher's chair.

—Kalli Dakos[2]

Since your students planned "what to do" with substitute teachers, this poem probably doesn't describe their experience! Still, all plans can have glitches, should be revisited periodically, and should be changed when necessary. This guideline offers an example of how to use a class meeting to check in on a specific event that students have anticipated (in this case, having a substitute teacher). In this meeting students have a chance to discuss how their time with a substitute went and, in light of that, to evaluate and perhaps modify the plan they created earlier.

Special Considerations • Hold the meeting after each time you have a substitute teacher in the classroom—by the end of the school year, the plan will be perfect!

The Class Meeting

Ideas for Opening the Meeting

■ **Explain the meeting purpose.**

Explain why it is important to take time to evaluate how well a plan actually worked.

■ **Have partners get the thinking started.**

Have students turn to a partner and identify one thing they liked about the day with the substitute and one problem that occurred.

Discussion Suggestions

■ **Invite students' reports of their experience with the substitute.**

Use questions such as those below to initiate an evaluation of the class's experience with the substitute:

• How did it go with the substitute?
   What were some good things that happened?
   Did anything surprising happen? Anything troubling or disappointing?
   Anything amusing?
   Were there any problems?

■ **Invite students' evaluation of their plan.**

Help students make connections between their plan and their experience with the substitute. You may find that young children, such as K–1 students, do not have the perspective-taking skills to engage in this conversation, and you will need to "lead" them to more conclusions than with older students. Use questions such as the following:

• How did our substitute plan help make the experience good for the class? How did it help make it good for the substitute?

   (Include in this discussion the use of any tools the class has created for substitute days, such as a Substitute's Handbook.*)*

• Do we need to make any changes in our plan? Did we leave anything out of our plan?

Record any suggestions, and help the class reach consensus on what changes (if any) to make in the plan and how to make them. For example, modifications might include adding specific information to the *Substitute's Handbook,* updating the seating chart or daily schedule, creating name tags or biographies for new class members, and so on.

■ **Establish responsibilities and a timeline.**

If changes or additions need to be made to any of the class's materials for substitutes, ask for volunteers to do so, and make sure they know how and when they will be able to do so.

Ideas for Concluding the Meeting

■ **Have students reflect on what they have learned about having a substitute.**

Help students summarize and draw conclusions about what they have learned. What have they learned about how they want a substitute to treat them? What have they learned about how they want to treat a substitute? What have they learned about how to achieve these results?

■ **Reread *Ramona the Pest.***

For K–1 students, reread Chapter 4 of *Ramona the Pest,* and ask students how their experience was similar to or different from Ramona's.

■ **Have students reflect on what they have learned about making plans.**

Ask students how it felt to review their plans. What did they learn about planning? How might this learning be important to them in the future?

■ **Have students evaluate the class meeting itself.**

Invite students' appraisal of various aspects of the meeting. Was there anything that went particularly well? Any problems? Any suggestions?

After the Meeting

To extend students' thinking about their experience with the substitute, choose one of the following activities.

■ **Letter to the Substitute**. Have the class write a letter to the substitute teacher, telling what they liked about the experience, what they learned from it, and changes they have made to their plan as a result.

■ **The Day the Substitute Came**. Have students write and/or illustrate serious or humorous stories about "The Day the Substitute Came," based on the things that surprised, disappointed, pleased, worried, or amused them about their experience with the substitute.

What's the Problem?

SOMETIMES it's enough to ask the question and let students talk about it with a check-in format. Sometimes a direct problem-solving approach is in order.

Problem Solving

GRADES K–6

An Outline of "Problem-Solving" Class Meetings

It is time for recess, and Ms. Lotz has instructed her first-grade class to put away their papers. Petra and Joyce vie for control of the file box that holds the work folders of students at their table group. "You're not the only one who needs to do it," protests Joyce with anger. "You're not the only one in this class that needs to learn!"

Around the room, other sharp remarks signal a widespread problem.

THIS guideline offers a general blueprint for using class meetings to address problems, both small and large, that confront teachers and their students. If used regularly, such class meetings can also help children acquire independent problem-solving and conflict resolution skills — skills they can use as a matter of course in resolving the daily conflicts that arise in the classroom, in the cafeteria, on the bus, on the playground, and outside of school, too.

The process suggested here consists of five basic steps:

1 Define the problem (in concrete terms that show why it is a problem that concerns everyone or that everyone can help with).

2 Generate solutions.

3 Discuss solutions.

4 Reach consensus.

5 Evaluate.

As you review the following suggestions for implementing these steps, you'll see that the suggestions allow considerable leeway for you to use your knowledge of your students and the specifics of the problem at hand to adapt this "blueprint" to your needs.

Before Your First Problem-Solving Meeting

■ **Post the steps.**

Translate the steps into readily accessible language, and post a list of the steps for reference during your meetings—and for students' use when they are solving problems on their own.

For example:

1 What's the problem?

2 Give ideas to fix it.

3 Discuss the ideas.

4 Choose one idea that's fair to all.

5 How did our idea work?

■ **If necessary, address "tattling."**

For younger children especially, you might need to differentiate between "tattling" and bringing a problem to the teacher as a genuine request for help. Unfortunately, the latter is often dismissed as tattling by children and adults alike, so it will benefit everyone to think about when and why students tell teachers about problems.

With the class, make a Venn diagram comparing tattling and asking a teacher to help with a problem. Encourage students to discuss the comparison. Throughout, be sure students understand that you *want* them to feel that they can bring problems to your attention and that this conversation is about doing so *responsibly*. (You might take the conversation even further and have students talk about when it is appropriate to seek the teacher's help, when students might work out problems themselves, and when the problem is one for the class to consider together in a meeting.)

■ **Practice the process.**

Before using this process to address a real classroom problem, hold a class meeting to introduce these conflict-resolution strategies to students, and have them practice the process on a few hypothetical problems. (Also keep in mind that every time students participate in a problem-solving class meeting, they are learning, practicing, and reinforcing their conflict-resolution skills.)

The Class Meeting

Ideas for Opening the Meeting

■ **Review recent problem-solving meetings.**

If students have participated in problem-solving meetings already, remind them of specific successes they have had in solving problems together. Likewise, if in previous problem-solving meetings students have identified aspects of the process that they need to work on, remind them of that resolve.

■ **Get children thinking about the type of problem at issue.**

Sometimes it may be useful to show a film or read a story that features the kind of problem to be addressed in the meeting; many children's books highlight common childhood and classroom problems. Or use other ways to start the meeting that uniquely suit the problem to be addressed. For example, the two class meeting guidelines that follow ("My Friends Won't Let Me Play" and "Cliques") open quite differently—one with a story, the other with an attention-getting exercise.

Discussion Suggestions

■ **Review the posted list of problem-solving steps.**

Review the list of steps, giving particular attention to Step One. Define the problem

- in *concrete* terms
- that show *why* it is a problem
- that *concerns everyone* or that everyone can help with.

■ **Step One: Define the Problem.**

Most meetings will start with a statement of a problem, either from you or from students, and the trick is to then help students recognize the underlying *cause* of the problem—they will often begin by citing only the symptoms. In order to find viable solutions, however, they will need to recognize the source of the problem, so encourage them to think through the issue in depth and from various angles. For example, in Ms. Lotz's class the problem between Petra and Joyce is a symptom of another problem that is causing trouble at other tables as well. Ms. Lotz could begin by simply stating, "I see that it is hard for us to get ready for recess. What's the problem?" The answers may range from "People are hogging the file box" to "Everyone is too slow" to "Some people won't clean up."

Probe such responses by asking some clarifying questions, such as the following:

- Why is this a problem?
- Who is it disturbing?
- Why do you think this is happening?

Such questioning can reveal what really needs to be resolved. For example, several table groups may need to make a specific plan for how they will get the papers filed, or the teacher may need to allow more time for the process, or both.

Keep students focused on the problem, not the perpetrators—but if the problem does involve "victims" and "victimizers," probe the feelings and motives associated with these "roles." Ask, for example:

- How does it feel to be teased (or called names, or pushed, etc.)?
- Why might a person tease someone else (or call names, or push, etc.)?

Encouraging this sort of perspective taking is important because it takes students beyond the prescriptive "don't-do-such-and-such" solutions and deepens their awareness of how their behavior affects others.

■ **Step Two: Generate Solutions.**

Have students brainstorm possible solutions to the problem, either as a whole class, in small groups, or in pairs. If the students work in groups, ask each group or partnership to share their ideas with the whole class. (Depending upon the topic and students' responsiveness or discussion skills, you will sometimes want to combine Steps Two and Three and discuss ideas as they are generated.)

■ **Step Three: Discuss Solutions.**

Talk over the benefits and burdens of each possible solution. Extend students' thinking about the nature and consequences of their proposed solutions, and help them see the connections between their ideas, by asking such questions as the following:

- Did anyone else have a similar idea?
- Does anyone have an idea that adds to this suggestion?
- Is this solution fair to everyone in the class?
- Can we change this idea to make it more fair or acceptable to everyone?

Judicious questions can help students identify the pitfalls in their own suggestions—unfair divisions of labor, approaches that will take too long or distract other students, punitive measures instead of long-term solutions, and so on.

■ **Step Four: Reach Consensus.**

The questions asked above will begin the consensus-building process by eliminating or modifying ideas through discussion. Another useful way to narrow the choices is to "test" the ideas by having students role-play the situation in which the problem arises and try out the proposed solutions. In each case, ask: Does the solution make sense? Are there any final adjustments required? Sometimes the best solution will prove to be a combination of students' ideas, and always the solution will be provisional—something to try, learn from, and perhaps rethink with experience. (See the "Consensus" section on pages 36–41 for other suggestions for helping students arrive at a decision.)

Finally, as mentioned earlier, some problems are addressed simply by airing them, heightening students' awareness of them, and having them propose many possible ways to solve or avoid them. Reaching consensus is not the goal in such instances.

Ideas for Concluding the Meeting

■ **Have students reflect on the meeting itself.**

Invite students to reflect on the usefulness of the meeting and how it went.

■ **Preview Step Five.**

Establish a time frame for evaluating the effectiveness of the solution(s) the class has proposed.

The Evaluation Meeting

■ **Step Five: Evaluate.**

Hold a check-in meeting to evaluate the class's progress in dealing with the problem or issue. If a new or revised solution is needed, begin again with Step One.

Follow-Up Activities

In addition to the evaluation class meeting, you might use the ideas below to reinforce students' appreciation of and commitment to their problem-solving efforts.

■ **Problem-Solving Book.** Begin a class book documenting problems that the class has faced and solved. Have students work in pairs to record in stories, cartoons, or drawings each problem and solution, and keep the "history" in a binder for students to add to throughout the year. The book is also useful for opening problem-solving meetings—by allowing you to refer back to earlier issues and problem-solving successes.

■ **Role-Play Replay.** After students have dealt with a problem successfully, ask them to role-play the problem and its solution for the benefit of the class.

My Friends Won't Let Me Play

GRADES K–2

Helping Children Become Problem Solvers

"A change for me has been class meetings—letting kids involved with conflicts talk things over and trying to stay out of it myself . . . Sometimes I have to help them with the words because their language isn't developed yet, but I don't any longer say things like 'I think you should go apologize.' I ask them to figure out what's right."

*L*IKE everyone else, young children have power struggles, which are sometimes expressed through name calling, put-downs, and excluding friends from play. These can be very upsetting incidents, and children may need help working through the conflict. Class meetings are one way to help children deal with their confusing or bad feelings and learn how to handle difficulties with friends. This guideline uses a fairly common childhood conflict—children being excluded from groups during free time—to give a specific example of using a conflict-resolution process with young children.

Special Considerations • Teachers need to be especially sensitive about using class meetings to address potentially emotional issues, such as being ignored by a friend, and should avoid holding meetings that single out specific individuals' conflicts. For example, you would not want to hold this meeting because of an incident between two children that should be dealt with privately—but if you notice a widespread or growing problem of children not including each other in their free play, you might use this class meeting to talk about it with all your students. Similarly, if you notice that certain children are consistently excluded from play because their attempts to be included are awkward or disruptive, you might want to help those children individually by teaching them some more successful strategies.

The Class Meeting

Ideas for Opening the Meeting

■ **Read a related story.**

"Open" the meeting the day before by reading aloud *Best Friends for Frances*, by Russell Hoban, and use the questions below to discuss the story and lead children into the class meeting topic. (While some of Frances's attempts to deal with her hurt feelings can't be recommended—name calling, tit-for-tat—they do represent fairly typical responses by children, and your conversation can help children distinguish between useful solutions and those that will only cause more hurt.) Encourage children to consider the feelings of the characters in the story by asking such questions as the following:

- How did Gloria feel when Frances wouldn't play ball with her and went to play with Albert instead? Why did she feel this way?

- How did Frances feel when Albert wouldn't have her along on his wandering day? Why did she feel this way?

- How did Gloria feel when Frances decided to play ball with her after all? How did Frances feel?

- Why do you think Frances let Albert go on the Best Friends' Outing?
  How do you think that made Frances feel?
  How do you think Albert would have felt if she hadn't let him come along?
  How do you think Albert felt when Frances included him?

Discussion Suggestions

■ **Step One: Define the Problem.**

Remind students of their earlier conversation about Frances, and use it to introduce the class meeting topic; for example: "We all seem to agree that Gloria and Frances and Albert felt bad when they were left out and were happier when they found ways to play together. But I think I've seen children leaving each other out during free time here at school—can we talk about that?"

■ **Have children remember a time they felt left out.**

Ask children to close their eyes for a moment and think about a time when they felt left out by a friend, and ask them to recall how they felt at the time (you may want to start by giving an example from your own childhood). Connect Frances's story and their own experiences to the class problem. For example:

- How did it feel when you were left out?

  (Try to steer the conversation away from "telling on" each other for specific slights, and focus it on the feelings they all experience at such times.)

- Why is it a problem when we leave classmates out during free time?
- Why do you think this is happening?

■ **Step Two: Generate Solutions.**

Have students work as a class, in small groups, or in partnerships to brainstorm ideas about what they could do when they feel as though they are being left out. If students have difficulty coming up with suggestions, get their thinking started by offering an idea or two of your own. For example:

- Ask someone else to play.
- Find something else to do.
- Ask a teacher or parent to help you talk to your friend.

■ **Step Three: Discuss Solutions.**

Help students reflect on each idea. If students offer overly general solutions (such as, "Everyone can start being nice to everybody else") or solutions that might escalate the conflict (such as, "I'd tell him I didn't really want to play with him anyway!"), use clarifying questions (such as "How would that help?") to help them elaborate or evaluate their responses. Record a class list of suggestions.

■ **Step Four: Reach Consensus.**

This is not the kind of problem that requires consensus on one solution. There should be consensus, however, that all the items on the list students generated are acceptable to everyone; have children revise the list if necessary.

Ideas for Concluding the Meeting

■ **Invite final comments about the list of suggestions.**

Ask if students have any questions or comments about the completed list or any conclusions to add to the discussion. Post the list where students can refer to it.

■ **Preview Step Five.**

Establish a time frame for evaluating the effectiveness of the solution(s) the class has proposed.

The Evaluation Meeting

■ **Step Five: Evaluate.**

Sometime later, hold a check-in meeting to consider how well the class is meeting their goal of not excluding people when they play. If necessary, have students redefine the problem and propose new ideas for addressing it.

*i*N ANY social or workplace group, individuals form closer bonds with some people than with others, and easily identifiable groups usually emerge. The extent to which those groups become exclusive, however, has broad and sometimes damaging consequences for the larger group. The purpose of this class meeting is to raise students' awareness of this (potential) issue, asking them to look at the ways in which formation of friendships can degenerate into excluding, scapegoating, and other harmful practices.

Special Considerations • Hold this meeting early in the year, before cliques have become a problem or resulted in serious hurts.

Cliques

GRADES 3–6

Helping Children Become Problem Solvers

The Class Meeting

Opening the Meeting

■ **Have students form a circle.**

Ask students to sit in a circle, anywhere they wish; most likely they will group themselves according to their friendships. Once seated, have them count off ("One," "Two," "Three," etc.) and then reseat themselves according to two rules:

- No one may sit next to anyone whose number is one or two above or below their own.

- Girls may not sit next to girls only, and boys may not sit next to boys only.

If students ask why you are rearranging the circle this way, tell them that you will explain later—which you will, if they don't figure it out themselves during the class discussion.

■ **Post the vocabulary chart.**

Introduce the class meeting topic by posting the following vocabulary chart and pointing out the "big category" definition that all three words have in common. Explain that you want to have a class discussion about ways we form friendships, or "small groups," that benefit the classroom community, and ways we form groups that can detract from the sense of community. Also explain that you will fill in the third column of the chart after the discussion.

Word	Big Category	Description/Uniqueness
A clique	is a small group of people	
Friends	are a small group of people	
A club	is a small group of people	

Discussion Suggestions

■ **Step One: Define the Problem.**

Begin by asking students what they think of when they hear the word "clique"; you will probably get a range of answers, but generally students will point to its association with snobbishness and rejection. If they aren't forthcoming with responses, suggest a general definition for the purposes of the discussion: for example, "Let's think of cliques as a group of special friends that stick together pretty much all the time—the group membership doesn't change."

■ **Discuss the benefits and burdens of cliques.**

Then use the following questions, or questions of your own, to help students think about the implications and problems of cliques in the classroom community.

• What are some benefits of cliques?
  Have you ever experienced a benefit of belonging to a special group?
  Why do you think people form cliques?

• Think about a time when you felt excluded from a special group. (Give students a minute for reflection.) Can you tell me what might be the burdens of cliques?
  Why do you think clique members don't let others into the group?

What are some burdens of being excluded from a special group?

What are some burdens of belonging to a special group?

Reflecting on these questions will help students "define the problem" of associating too narrowly or exclusively with a small group of people—the negative consequences for clique members, those they reject, and the larger community.

■ **Steps Two and Three: Generate and Discuss Solutions.**

Use such questions as the following to help students think through their response to cliques:

• What can we do in our class to keep friendships and interest groups from becoming cliques?

What can students do?

What can I (the teacher) do?

• Why do you think I asked you to move from your original place in the circle?

What were the advantages of moving?

What were the disadvantages of moving?

■ **Step Four: Reach Consensus.**

In this discussion you won't be reaching consensus on a solution, but on a shared understanding of when friendship groups can do more harm than good. If necessary, make sure that students understand that you aren't asking every class member to be equally and mutually close friends—but that you want them to be careful not to forge the bonds of friendship at others' (painful) expense.

Ideas for Concluding the Meeting

■ **Complete the chart.**

Help students reflect on their conversation by completing the vocabulary chart with the class.

Word	Big Category	Description/Uniqueness
A clique	is a small group of people	who exclude others.
Friends	are a small group of people	who like one another.
A club	is a small group of people	who have a similar interest.

Ask if students have any questions or comments about the completed vocabulary chart or any conclusions to add to the discussion.

■ **Have students reflect on the class meeting itself.**

Invite students to reflect on the usefulness of the meeting and how it went.

■ **Preview Step Five.**

Establish a time frame for evaluating how well the class is avoiding cliquishness.

The Evaluation Meeting

■ **Step Five: Evaluate.**

Sometime later, hold a check-in class meeting about cliques. Ask students to evaluate how well their earlier understandings about cliques and friendships have helped them make the classroom a place where being friends doesn't mean hurting others. If necessary, have students redefine the problem and propose new ideas for addressing it.

Follow-Up Activities

■ **Preventive Measures.** Find (or create) opportunities to use community-building activities and cooperative learning configurations to help deter cliquishness in the classroom.

■ **Read All about It.** Read aloud to the class a story that deals with this topic in some way, such as Eleanor Estes's *The Hundred Dresses,* and have students discuss the ideas about cliques that it raises.

Class Meeting Checklist

Below is a quick summary of key points that you may want to consider as you plan, execute, and evaluate meetings for your classroom community.

Setting the agenda for planning or decision-making meetings

☐ Is the topic open-ended (or do I have a predetermined solution)?

☐ Am I willing to let students act on their ideas?

Setting a routine for daily or weekly check-in meetings

☐ Do students understand that this is a time to reflect on what we are learning and what we would like to learn?

☐ Do students understand that this is an opportunity to reflect on and perhaps revise previous decisions and plans?

☐ Do students understand that this is a time to celebrate successes?

☐ Do students understand that these meetings are not just a venue for airing complaints, but that they might try other solutions before bringing problems to these meetings?

Setting the agenda for consciousness-raising or problem-solving meetings

☐ Is this a topic that feels "safe"? Have students had enough experience with each other? With me? Is there danger of this meeting turning into a "kangaroo court"?

☐ Is this a topic better addressed by a small group (or the group immediately concerned)?

☐ Have the concerned parties all agreed to have this problem taken to the class? Are they all present?

☐ Is this the best time for this meeting?

Setting the environment

☐ Have students had adequate opportunities to get to know and feel comfortable with one another?

☐ Do students understand the ground rules? Do we need to review them?

☐ Do students understand that all ideas are valued ("no put-downs")?

☐ Are there certain students with whom I should have special signals?

☐ Can students see and hear one another easily?

☐ Have I allowed enough time for the meeting so that students will not feel cut off or hurried? Am I prepared to end the meeting early if students show little interest in the topic?

☐ Do students understand that not every meeting will have a resolution?

Encouraging discussion

☐ Do I model interested listening behavior?

☐ Do I ask open-ended questions?

☐ Do I model how to get more information from a respondent?

☐ Do I model how to make connections between ideas?

☐ Am I able to wait in silence for students to think about their answers?

☐ Am I able to rephrase (or drop) questions that fail to stimulate discussion?

☐ Do students feel safe expressing their own ideas, as opposed to ideas they think I want to hear?

☐ Do students understand that they do not have to address their ideas to the teacher? Am I encouraging students to respond directly to one another?

☐ Do students understand they will not be put on the spot to answer? Have I given them various opportunities to participate, other than whole-group discussion?

☐ Do students know the rules of "brainstorming" (i.e., offer any idea and reserve comment for now)?

☐ Are students comfortable talking with a partner or in small groups to get their thinking started?

☐ Are students comfortable talking with a partner or in small groups if there are more ideas than opportunity to hear them all in a whole-class discussion?

☐ Might students benefit from individual writing and reflection to focus or "cool down" their arguments?

Building consensus

☐ Do students understand what consensus is?

☐ Do students understand why we try to reach consensus rather than just vote?

☐ Do students understand that consensus can be hard to achieve?

☐ Do students understand when it is better to reach consensus than hold on to an idea? Do they know how to combine ideas, alter ideas, compromise?

☐ Am I comfortable ending an unproductive meeting and returning to the topic later?

☐ When the class reaches consensus, am I helping students appreciate their accomplishment?

Evaluating decisions of problem-solving meetings

☐ Do students understand that we will always review our decisions to see whether or how to adjust or revise them?

☐ When's the last time we did this?

Encouraging reflection

☐ Do I leave enough time to review the meeting? (Note: K–1 students might not be quite ready for meaningful reflection, but other grades should always incorporate reflection into class meetings.)

☐ Do I encourage students to reflect on process and outcomes and to suggest thoughtful revisions?

As you evaluate your process and results, always remember that (1) not every meeting will turn out as you might have wanted or expected, (2) it takes time for teacher and students—facilitator and participants—to master the class-meeting process, and (3) the process itself is valuable. As one teacher said, upon observing a fellow teacher's class meeting:

> **"His class meeting was a worse bust than any class meeting I've ever had . . . yet he felt he got something out of it in terms of changes that he could make in his classroom. It spurred me on to realize that I could get something out of class meetings even if they don't turn out perfectly."**

Teacher Support Materials from
Developmental Studies Center

Among Friends: Classrooms Where Caring and Learning Prevail
In classroom vignettes and conversations with teachers across the country, this 208-page book provides concrete ideas for building caring learning communities in elementary school classrooms. With a focus on how the ideas of the research-based Child Development Project (CDP) play out in practice, Australian educator Joan Dalton and CDP Program Director Marilyn Watson take us into classrooms where teachers make explicit how they promote children's intellectual, social, and ethical development simultaneously throughout the day and across the curriculum. A chapter on theory and research provides a coherent rationale for the approach teachers demonstrate.

At Home in Our Schools
The 136-page book focuses on schoolwide activities that help educators and parents create caring school communities. It includes ideas about leadership, step-by-step guidelines for 15 activities, and reproducible planning resources and suggestions for teachers. The 12-minute overview video is designed for use in staff meetings and PTO/parent gatherings to create support for a program of whole-school activities. The 48-page study guide structures a series of organizing meetings for teachers, parents, and administrators.

The Collegial Study Package includes the book, the overview video, and the study guide.

Blueprints for a Collaborative Classroom
This "how-to" collection of partner and small-group activities is organized into 25 categories that cover the waterfront—from a quick partner interview to a complex research project. Over 200 activity suggestions are included for all elementary grades, in categories like Mindmapping, Decision-Making, Partner Reading, Editing, and Investigating. In addition, Fly-on-the-Wall vignettes offer insights from real classrooms. (176 pages)

Choosing Community: Classroom Strategies for Learning and Caring
In nine videotaped presentations, author and lecturer Alfie Kohn describes pivotal choices that promote community and avoid coercion and competition in classrooms. A 64-page facilitator's guide for use in staff development accompanies the presentations, which include such topics as "The Case Against Competition," "The Consequences of 'Consequences,'" "The Trouble with Rewards," and "Beyond Praise and Grades." The package also includes Kohn's influential book *Punished by Rewards: The Trouble with Gold Stars, Incentive Plans, A's, Praise and Other Bribes.*

Homeside Activities (K–5)
Six separate collections of activities by grade level help teachers, parents, and children communicate. Each 128-page collection has an introductory overview, 18 reproducible take-home activities in English and Spanish, and suggestions for teachers on integrating the activities into the life of the classroom. The 12-minute overview video is designed for use at parent gatherings and staff meetings as an overview of a program of Homeside Activities. The 48-page study guide structures a series of teacher meetings for collegial study inservice.

The Collegial Study Package includes one each K–5 books, the overview video, the study guide, and a 31-minute video documenting 3 classrooms and parents working at home with their children.

Number Power (Grades K–6)
Each 192-page teacher resource book offers three replacement units (8–12 lessons per unit) that foster students' mathematical and social development. Students collaboratively investigate problems, develop their number sense, enhance their mathematical reasoning and communication skills, and learn to work together effectively.

Reading, Thinking & Caring: Literature-Based Reading (Grades K–3)

A children's literature program to help students love to read, think deeply and critically, and care about how they treat themselves and others. Teaching units are available for over 80 classic, contemporary, and multicultual titles. Each 3- to 10-day unit includes a take-home activity in English and Spanish to involve parents in their children's life at school. Also available are grade-level sets and accompanying trade books.

Reading for Real: Literature-Based Reading (Grades 4–8)

A literature-based program to engage the student's conscience while providing interesting and important reading, writing, speaking, and listening experiences. Teaching units are available for over 100 classic, contemporary, and multi-cultural titles, and each 1- to 3-week unit includes a take-home activity to involve parents in children's life at school. Also available are grade-level sets and accompanying trade books.

Reading for Real Collegial Study

Videotaped classroom vignettes illustrate key concepts and common stumbling blocks in facilitating literature-based classroom discussion. A 64-page study guide structures a series of five collegial study meetings that cover the following topics: "Reflecting and Setting Goals," "Responding to Students," "Handling Offensive Comments and Sensitive Topics," "Guiding Students' Partner Discussions," and "Assessing Student Progress."

That's My Buddy! Friendship and Learning Across the Grades

The 140-page book is a practical guide for two buddy teachers or a whole staff. It draws on the experiences of teachers from DSC's Child Development Project schools across the country. The 12-minute overview video is designed for use at staff meetings to build interest in a schoolwide buddies program. The 48-page study guide structures a series of teacher meetings for collegial study and support once a buddies program is launched.

The Collegial Study Package includes the book, the overview video, and the study guide.

Ways We Want Our Class To Be: Class Meetings That Build Commitment to Kindness and Learning

The 116-page book describes how to use class meetings to build a caring classroom community and address the academic and social issues that arise in the daily life of the elementary school classroom. In addition to tips on getting started, ground rules, and facilitating the meetings, 14 guidelines for specific class meetings are included. The 20-minute overview video visits a variety of class meetings in grades K–5/6 and includes teacher interviews. The Class Meetings Package includes the book; the overview video; a 48-page study guide to help structure a series of teacher meetings for collegial study; and three additional videos documenting seven classrooms where students are involved in planning and decision making, checking in on learning and behavior, and problem solving.

The Collegial Study Package includes the book, the overview video, the study guide, and 99 minutes of video documenting 7 classrooms.

For ordering information:

Publications Department
Developmental Studies Center
2000 Embarcadero, Suite 305
Oakland, CA 94606-5300
(800) 666-7270 • (510) 533-0213